D1426442

D. H. LAWRENCE AND THE ART OF TRANSLATION

D. H. LAWRENCE AND THE ART OF TRANSLATION

G. M. Hyde

First published by
MACMILLAN PRESS LTD
Houndmills, Basingstoke, Hampshire RG21 6XS
and London
Companies and representatives
throughout the world

ISBN 0-333-28599-9

A catalogue record for this book is available from the British Library.

This book is printed on paper suitable for recycling and made from fully managed and sustained forest sources.

Transferred to digital printing 1999

Printed in Great Britain by
Antony Rowe Ltd, Chippenham, Wiltshire

I would like to express thanks to the University
of Essex for the research award which made possible
the work on which this book is based

Contents

Acknowledgements

The author and publishers are grateful to The Hogarth Press Limited for permission to quote from *The Gentleman from San Fransisco* by Ivan Bunin from the volume *The Gentleman from San Fransisco and Other Stories*, translated by S. S. Koteliansky, D. H. Lawrence and Leonard Woolf.

Every effort has been made to trace all the copyright holders but if any have been inadvertently overlooked the publishers will be pleased to make the necessary arrangement at the first opportunity.

Preface

This study is concerned with the translations of D. H. Lawrence from Italian and Russian. The are undeniably a very minor part of a major *oeuvre*, yet they do not deserve the almost complete neglect they have been accorded. At the present moment it is difficult even to get hold of texts of some of them. The Grove Press edition of *Mastro-Don Gesualdo*, for example, is currently unobtainable, and it is in any case not a new edition but reproduced from the plates of the Seltzer first edition, misprints and all. The Penguin editions are currently out of print. The translation from Lasca, *The Story of Dr Manente*, has not been reissued since the first edition published in Florence, and the London edition of P. E. Grey from the following year (February 1930). Warren Roberts records that the Italian publisher, Orioli, mentions[1] that his successors in the business still had copies on their hands as late as 1957. Had these been copies of an original work by Lawrence, these first editions would not have stayed on a publisher's shelf for nearly thirty years. But they were not: they were "merely" translations. Lawrence's translation of Bunin's *The Gentleman from San Francisco*, however, was reprinted in *Phoenix Two* (1968).

Copies of Lawrence's translations are hard to find, perhaps because they have not come to be accepted as part of the Lawrence canon. Moreover the authors Lawrence chose to translate lacked classic status. He backed a loser in translating Verga. His prefaces, which I examine in detail later, show that he was battling with public taste in attempting to establish the greatness of this very great author with an English public which had recently discovered the Russian masters, and found Verga crude. Modern Italian literature had always been rather beyond the pale in England. The translations from the Russian might have been expected to fare better. But Lawrence never managed to read Russian,[2] so he worked always in collaboration and in fact translated little. The short story by the Russian émigré writer Ivan Bunin that he chose to translate in collaboration with his close friend S. S. Koteliansky can be shown, I believe, to contain a great deal of Lawrence's own work. Thereafter we are more in the dark. It is symptomatic of a regrettably widespread disrespect for the translation process that it is still not entirely possible to be sure of where, among all the vast output of the 1920s and 1930s Russianists, one can find evidence of Lawrence's hand. In the Warren Roberts bibliography, which is usually sure of its facts, we find speculation. Under entry A.13, for example, *"All Things are Possible" by Leo Shestov, with a foreword by D. H. Lawrence*, Roberts writes as follows:

Although Lawrence is credited only with the 'foreword' for this translation of Shestov's *All Things are Possible*, Bertram Rota reports that S. S. Koteliansky named D. H. Lawrence as a full collaborator in the translation. Koteliansky was a member of the Lawrence coterie [*sic*] during the war years in England, and he remained a friend and literary associate of Lawrence's. Apparently Koteliansky felt that he did not write English well enough to carry through the work of translation without assistance. J. M. Murry collaborated with him on several translations before Lawrence agreed to work on *All Things are Possible*. The final translation was effected through a complete revision by Lawrence of Koteliansky's version. Koteliansky's original manuscript was so heavily revised that Lawrence eventually rewrote the entire translation in his own handwriting; this was the manuscript from which Secker printed the present edition.

Why, then, did Lawrence's name not appear on this volume

(except, that is, for the Preface)? The letters in the Koteliansky collection in the British Library, edited by George J. Zytaruk under the title *The Quest for Rananim*,[3] provide an answer. In a letter of 1918 (or possibly 1919) Lawrence writes:

> I don't want my name printed as a translator. It won't do for me to appear to dabble in too many things. If you don't want to appear alone — but why shouldn't you? — put me a nom de plume like Richard Ham or Thomas Ball. Also, when it comes to payment, in mere justice my part is one-third. Don't argue this with me. If you are a Shestovian, accept the facts . . . Please go through my version, and alter anything you think fit.

Although Lawrence talks here of "dabbling", the rest of the letters to Koteliansky in connection with this translation record unremitting hard work. Lawrence never dabbled, and it should not be deduced from his caginess here that he did not respect the translator's art. In what is probably his only extended public comment on the translation process, a section of his essay on *Pedro de Valdivia* by R. B. Cunninghame Graham,[4] a volume which contains translations of some of Pedro's letters, Lawrence speaks harshly of Graham's laxity in his renderings of them:

> Then we have Mr. Graham as a translator. In the innumerable and sometimes quite fatuous and irritating footnotes — they are sometimes interesting — our author often gives the original Spanish for the phrase he has translated. And even here he is peculiarly glib and unsatisfactory: ' "God knows the trouble it cost," he says pathetically'. Valdivia is supposed to say this 'pathetically'. The footnote gives Valdivia's words: "Un bergantin y el trabajo qué costó. Dios lo sabe." — "A brigantine, and the work it cost, God knows." Why 'trouble' for 'trabajo'? and why 'pathetically'? Again, the proverb: 'A Dios rogando, y con la maza dando' is translated: 'Praying to God, and battering with the mace.'

But why 'battering' for 'dando', which means merely 'don-
nant', and might be rendered 'smiting' or 'laying on', but
surely not 'battering'! Again, Philip II is supposed to say to
Ercilla, who stammered so much as to be unintelligible,
'Habladme por escrito, Don Alonso!' Which is: 'Say it to me
in writing, Don Alonso!' Mr. Graham, however, translates
it: 'Write to me, Don Alonso!' . . . These things are trifles,
but they show the peculiar laziness or insensitiveness to
language which is so great a vice in a translator.

The motto of the book is

'El más seguro don de la fortuna
Es no lo haber tenido vez alguna.'

Mr. Graham puts it: 'The best of fortune's gifts is never to
have had good luck at all.' Well, Ercilla may have meant this.
The literal sense of the Spanish, anybody can make out:
'The most sure gift of fortune, is not to have had it not
once.' Whether one would be justified in changing the 'don
de la fortuna' of the first line into 'good luck' in the second
is a point we must leave to Mr. Graham. Anyhow, he seems
to have blest his own book in this equivocal fashion.

Lawrence himself, whatever the faults of his translations,
never showed "laziness and insensitiveness to language".
Indeed in this essay he seems to be calling for the greatest
possible fidelity to the original text, and his own practice as
a translator bears this out: it is a question not simply of being
literal but of responding to the distinctive "otherness" of the
patterns of thought and feeling a foreign language embodies.[5]
His remarks on the nature of the Italian language, in his essay
on Grazia Deledda's novel *The Mother*, may be of questionable
validity as descriptive linguistics (Lawrence adopts a position
which one might classify as an exceptionally "monadic" version of the Whorf-Sapir hypothesis[6]) but are evidence of the
acute, possibly exaggerated, feeling of that "otherness" of a
foreign language:

The book, of course, loses a good deal in translation, as is inevitable. In the mouths of the simple people, Italian is a purely instinctive language, with the rhythm of instinctive rather than mental processes. There are also many instinct-words with meanings never clearly mentally defined. In fact, nothing is brought to real mental clearness, everything goes by in a stream of more or less vague, more or less realized, feeling, with a natural mist or glow of sensation over everything, that counts more than the actual words said; and which, alas, it is almost impossible to reproduce in the more cut-and-dried northern languages, where every word has its fixed value and meaning, like so much coinage. A language can be killed by over precision, killed especially as an effective medium for the conveyance of instinctive passion and instinctive emotion. One feels this, reading a translation from the Italian. And though Grazia Deledda is not masterly as Giovanni Verga is, yet, in Italian at least, she can put us into the mood and rhythm of Sardinia, like a true artist, an artist whose work is sound and enduring.

The remarks on Italy and Italian are not, in themselves, original; indeed, we may see here a well-established Anglo-Saxon attitude to Italian "naivety"; yet this quotation raises larger issues, still relevant to the theme of translation, bound up with the question, for example, of what drew Lawrence to Italian literature rather than any other (he was as well equipped linguistically to translate French or German or Spanish, at different stages of his life). This is a question, ultimately, of the function of the spiritual-symbolic domain and the geographic reality of "Italy" as country and as concept in Lawrence's peculiar psychic universe; and it can hardly be answered without reference to the question of how this country of the mind coexists and interacts with the more complex and ambivalent nervous "projection" of Russia and the Russian literary tradition.[7] The Koteliansky papers have shown at last how strong was the pull of Russia — in addition to the fascination of Russian literature — for Lawrence: through his letters to Koteliansky we can trace his intermittent impulses towards her, even to the extent of his several times thinking of going there as to a promised land, his "Rananim".[8] These impulses were followed by equally violent recoils. At the same time, he made several, apparently unsuccessful, attempts to learn Russian. As to literary influence, of course, there has never been any doubt, and Zytaruk's recent book, comprehensive as it is, seems still to leave room for further study.[9] Lawrence's frequent bouts of antipathy to things Russian (coloured by his antipathy to the English Russianists, and the complications of his friendship with Murry) cannot obscure the enormous importance of Russian literature in Lawrence's own thinking and writing. It is in this connection that the Shestov translation rewards study, and from this point of view, primarily, that I discuss it. It would be interesting to take up this subject with regard to Rozanov, too: for perhaps Lawrence had a hand in the translation of *Fallen Leaves* and *Solitaria* (there are some grounds for the claim that is sometimes made that Rozanov played a part in the shaping of the eroticism of Lawrence's last works); but it seems impossible to prove it. Indeed, the wild goose chase started by Bertram Rota (as recorded by Warren Roberts) still has repercussions:

> In a memo. dated 28 April 1952, Mr. Rota writes, 'Koteliansky says the reason why Lawrence's name does not appear as a collaborator in the translation of this book [i.e. Shestov] or of Dostoyevsky's *Grand Inquisitor* or other translations which they did together, is that Lawrence felt it would be damaging to his reputation with publishers as a creative writer if he should appear as a translator.[10]

The fact that the latter part of this statement can now be shown to be true, and that the claim with reference to Shestov is also proven, does not mean that the rest holds water: critical analysis of, for example, the Dostoyevsky text seems to me inconclusive.

My task, for the present, is less ambitious. It is to examine

closely those translations which are beyond doubt by Lawrence, or to which he made an extensive and well-authenticated
contribution; to attempt to determine what factors, intrinsic
and extrinsic, prompted him to undertake these translations;
to justify the sense I have, and the claims I shall make, that
all Lawrence's translations are, whatever their faults, artistic
works of a high order of distinction;[11] and to indicate what
kind of gain there may be for Lawrence's own writing arising
from the fact of his close engagement with foreign languages
and literatures, that quality which, for all his much-stressed
Englishness, demanded the resistance of alien tongues, texts,
and traditions, making him a European writer in a very
important sense, as many of his English contemporaries were
not.

A full list of the editions I have worked from is appended
in a short bibliography. It has proved difficult to establish
exactly which edition of particular texts Lawrence worked
from. The order of the stories in the *Vita dei Campi*[12] collection proves that it was not the first edition, but the second,
where Verga has placed the very popular *Cavalleria Rusticana*
first, by way of advertising his wares; but (as Cecchetti points
out) he luckily did not get hold of the later editions, current
in the 1930s, which incorporate Verga's unfortunate revisions,
all of which are aimed at greater smoothness and stylistic
polish, smudging the harsh integrity and terseness characteristic of his genius. The text of *Mastro-Don Gesualdo* from which
Lawrence worked is evidently in essence identical to that of
the modern edition, published by Mondadori, from which I
worked: any discrepancies are surely fortuitous. There seems
to be no textual problem with the Grazzini: the first edition
that came to hand corresponds exactly to Lawrence's version.
The Bunin text is more problematic: at first sight, it seems as
if there are a large number of significant departures from the
Russian in the Koteliansky/Lawrence version. But in fact the
text Koteliansky used must have been that of the émigré
edition published in Paris in 1920, which is longer and (to my
mind) richer and subtler than the text now published in

Soviet editions: which give no indication that they are not printing the text of the first edition (St Petersburg, 1915). The Paris text may well be a revision of the first edition. The changes made, as I have said, in contradistinction to Verga's second thoughts, do not seem to weaken the text but to strengthen it. A few minor discrepancies between the Paris text and the Hogarth Press edition of Lawrence's translation crept in after the text was printed in *The Dial*;[13] they quite probably represent minor revisions made without reference to the original. But in view of the episodic nature of the translation process in this case, the degree of verbal fidelity to the original is remarkable. It would have been otiose to analyse the Russian text of Shestov's *All Things Are Possible* (*Apofeoz Bezpochvennosti*, St Petersburg, 1905) with the same close attention I give to the Bunin text, since it holds quite a different kind of interest for the student of Lawrence. I have therefore cited passages from the Russian only where a discrepancy between it and Lawrence's English can be interpreted with reasonable certainty as evidence that Lawrence is passing judgement on (or wilfully misreading) Shestov's arguments, with which he was not entirely in sympathy.

Before passing on to the main body of this work, I would like to call attention to one more, and in this case very elusive, aspect of Lawrence's work as a translator. Some of his early poems, which are included in the *Collected Poems*[14] in slightly revised forms, are translations of German versions of Arabic "fellah" (demotic) texts, mainly, it seems, the lyrics of love songs. While staying with his uncle, Fritz Krenkow, Lawrence translated these poems from a volume[15] that he found in the library of Krenkow, who was an Arabic scholar. The original versions of these translations, often much corrected and in the form of rough drafts, are included in letters to Louise Burrows of 1910 and 1911,[16] that is, at the time of Lawrence's short-lived engagement to her. It is clear that Lawrence uses them, as translators commonly use the foreign texts they select, as "masks" to express sentiments he would be reluctant to utter in person: in this way they both reveal and conceal how he "really" felt about Louise, who does not seem₁ to have engaged his deepest feelings. Lawrence paid court to Louise, to some extent, through these Arabic poems, and discarded them when they had served their purposes (Letter 246), though he thought them worth revising and preserving later. Any more systematic commentary on these translations has been frustrated by the impossibility of tracing the originals (cf. *Letters* Vol. I, p. 196), though probably their interest would be very marginal.

NOTES

(The Notes in this book give full bibliographical details only for those publications not listed in the Select Bibliography)

1. Giuseppe Orioli, *Adventures of a Bookseller*, cited in Warren Roberts's *Bibliography of the Works of D. H. Lawrence* (London: Soho Bibliographies 1963).
2. He made more than one attempt, as his *Letters* reveal.
3. George J. Zytaruk, *The Quest for Rananim*.
4. Edward D. McDonald (ed.), *Phoenix: The Posthumous Papers of D. H. Lawrence*.
5. Cf. Walter Benjamin, "The Task of the Translator" in *Illuminations* (London: Cape, 1973).
6. John B. Carroll (ed.), *Language, Thought and Reality: Selected Writings of Benjamin Lee Whorf* (New York: Wiley, 1956).
7. Cf. George J. Zytaruk, *D. H. Lawrence's Response to Russian Literature*.
8. The name originates with the Hebrew chant which Koteliansky used to sing.
9. Helen Muchnic, in *Dostoevsky's English Reputation* (Northampton, Mass: Smith College, 1939), does not go deep enough. Essays by Henry Gifford, F. R. Leavis and Raymond Williams have suggested analogies between Lawrence and Tolstoy.
10. Warren Roberts, op. cit.
11. My understanding of the aesthetics of translation rests inevitably upon George Steiner's definitive study, *After Babel*.
12. There are no significant textual differences.
13. January 1922.
14. V. da Sola Pinto and Warren Roberts (eds.), *The Collected Poems of D. H. Lawrence* (New York: Smith College, 1964).
15. This volume has proved impossible to trace.
16. J. T. Boulton (ed.), *The Letters of D. H. Lawrence* (Cambridge: CUP, 1979).

1 Lawrence, Italy and Russia, with an examination of Shestov's *All Things are Possible*

In Chapter 6 of his study of Lawrence's critical writings, *D. H. Lawrence as a Literary Critic*,[1] which is entitled 'Heroes of Death and Heroes of Rebirth', D. J. Gordon comments at some length on Lawrence's vivid response to foreign countries and foreign cultures:

> Italy was always dear to Lawrence, but for the reasons indicated, he did not pursue his thought-adventure very ardently through Italian culture. Nor, for different reasons, did he particularly interest himself in either French or German culture. He was always more or less hostile to the French spirit; it seemed too rationalised and sophisticated to be either lovely in itself, like the Italian, or promising for the future, like the Russian and American.

"The reasons indicated" consist in the special role of Verga's writings in Lawrence's imaginative cosmos: they constitute, that is, a vision of a world both Homeric and modern (Lawrence's own characterisation) or, to adopt D. J. Gordon's terminology, "a pre-falled imaginative world". As such, despite their great significance in a "utopian" scheme of things, or in terms of Lawrence's theology of Love and Law,[2] they have a limited part to play in the formulation of an aesthetic adequate to the expression and transcendence of the contemporary crisis. Or as Lawrence himself puts it, more crisply, in his foreword to *Studies in Classic American Literature*: "Two bodies of modern literature have come to a real verge: the Russian and the American."

The brink of contemporary chaos was reached, Lawrence thought, in Dostoevsky: yet it seemed to him (and he later believed that he found support for his view in Shestov, though this involved a certain degree of misreading) that Dostoevsky did not go beyond this, to the new consciousness implicit in the crisis. As inportant letter to Murry, written during Lawrence's nightmare year (1916),[3] elaborates upon this notion:

> An epoch of the human mind may have come to the end in Dostoevsky: but humanity is capable of going on a very long way further yet, in a state of mindlessness — curse it. And you've got the cart before the horse. It isn't the being that must follow the mind, but the mind must follow the being. And if only the cursed cowardly world had the courage to follow its own being with its mind, if it only had the courage to know what its unknown *is*, its own desires and its own activities, it might get beyond to the new secret. But the trick is, when you draw somewhere near the 'brink of revelation', to dig your head in the sand like the disgusting ostrich, and see the revelation there. Meanwhile, with their heads in the sand of pleasing visions and secrets and revelations, they kick and squirm with their behinds, most disgustingly. I don't blame humanity for having no mind, I blame it for putting its mind in a box and using it as a nice little self-gratifying instrument. You've got to know, and know everything, before you 'transcend' into the 'unknown'. But Dostoevsky, like the rest, can nicely stick his head between the feet of Christ, and waggle his behind in the air. And though the behind-wagglings are a revelation, I don't think much even of the feet of Christ, as a bluff for the cowards to hide their eyes against . . . [4]

The pointing out of the way to the new is left for Shestov, a

minor Existentialist (he can be shown to have influenced
Camus), and to Rozanov, two important works by whom, in
translations by Koteliansky, Lawrence wrote about at some
length towards the end of his life, finding in them the kind of
originality to which the Russian critic Victor Shklovsky (whose
work Lawrence probably did not know of) had already
drawn attention in his book *Sjuzhet kak yavlenie stilya*
(Petrograd: Opoyaz, 1921). At all events, Lawrence's letters
and essays bear witness to a lifelong engagement, or running
battle, with Russian literature and English Russianists; whereas Italian literature as a whole interested him little, so that he
could write to E. M. Brewster from Sicily in November 1921:
"I have been reading Giovanni Verga's Sicilian novels and
stories. Do you know them? When one gets into his really
rather difficult style (to me), he is very interesting. The only
Italian who does interest me."

Lawrence's passionate concern for Russian literature was
present from his youth onwards, as Jessie Chambers's memoirs
show (*D. H. Lawrence: Personal Record* (Cape, 1935)): and
by 1914 his knowledge was great enough for him to begin to
construct his general critique of the moral order of the great
Russian novels, which he lumps together too readily: "The
certain moral scheme is what I object to. In Turgenev, and in
Tolstoi, and in Dosteovsky, the moral scheme into which all
the characters fit — and it is nearly the same scheme — is,
whatever the extraordinariness of the characters themselves,
dull, old, dead." This is followed by the well-known praise of
Marinetti and Italian Futurism. Peremptory though it may
be, Lawrence's over-view of Russian literature has a kind of
significance when seen in terms of his impatience with the
"Russianitis" already beginning to set in in fashionable intellectual circles, which was often shallow, poorly informed,
and undiscriminating. There is no doubt that one of the most
attractive qualities that Lawrence found in Verga was his
freedom from "coruscating souls" (a phrase used in connection with Russian literature and its advocates in Lawrence's
preface to *Mastro-Don Gesualdo*[5]). Lawrence is, in fact, quite

explicit in his enlisting of Verga against the hated Bloomsbury "enlightenment" (though it would of course be misleading to suggest that he is just "using" Verga in some kind of cross-cultural feud):

> How utterly different it is from Russia, where the people are always — in the books — expanding to one another, and pouring out tea and their souls to one another all night long. In Sicily, by nightfall, nearly every man is barricaded inside his own house. Save in the hot summer, when the night is more or less turned into day.
>
> It all seems, to some people, dark and squalid and brutal and boring. There is no soul, no enlightenment at all. There is not one single enlightened person. If there had been, he would have departed long ago. He could not have stayed.
>
> And for people who seek enlightenment, oh, how boring! But if you have any physical feeling for life, apart from nervous feelings such as the Russians have, nerves, nerves, if you have any appreciation for the southern way of life, then, what a strange, deep fascination there is in *Mastro-Don Gesualdo*.

There is an equivocal note here, as elsewhere in the same essay, deriving from the characteristically Lawrentian identification of literature with life, his refusal to postulate a sophisticated recording consciousness — "If there had been [an enlightened man] . . . '. The setting up of Verga (undeniably a conscious artist) as such a strong "Homeric" positive places Lawrence in an awkward position, and one which he seems to realise is not altogether tenable. Modern man is, he knows, a super-conscious animal, and has no choice in the matter: the disease gnawing him is more comprehensive than the "dog" eating Don Gesualdo's liver; and the diagnosis of this disease, without which there can be no "cure", lies with the Russians. In declaring that Russian literature had come to a "verge", Lawrence admitted as much, however reluctantly, and there can be no doubt of his fascination with Dosteovsky, for whom he felt, as he admitted, a kind of "subterranean love". And as I have said it seemed to him intermittently that there was some hope of something new and better in the political reality of the Soviet state as well as in that country of the mind which had been through the conflagration and was waiting to be born again as a Lawrentian phoenix. My emphasis therefore will be on Russia, in this chapter, leaving Italy for Chapters 2 and 3.

The collection of letters bequeathed to the British Museum in 1955 by S. S. Koteliansky, subsequently edited and published by G. J. Zytaruk,[6] has made it possible for the first time to trace in detail the complex flow and recoil of sympathy Lawrence felt Russia and Russian literature, an aspect of his activities to which little attention had previously been given. Koteliansky ("Kot") was one of Lawrence's most valued and reliable friends, with whom (and this makes him most unusual) Lawrence never fell out. He was a Russian Jew, born in the Ukraine in 1880, who came to England in 1911 on a three-months study grant, and stayed permanently, moving largely in Bloomsbury circles but not, like many others, as a camp follower: his independence was without doubt one of the qualities Lawrence most admired in him. He received over three hundred letters from Lawrence, whom he had helped in many ways (the earliest letters refer to the typing of the manuscript of Lawrence's *Study of Thomas Hardy*, and towards the end of Lawrence's life he helped most ably and courageously in the marketing of *Lady Chatterley's Lover*, Lawrence being at the time in Italy). Lawrence borrowed certain superficial traits from Koteliansky for the character of Kangaroo in the novel of the same name, and it is interesting to note that it was from Koteliansky that Lawrence took the name of his ideal state of the future, Rananim: this word, which surely suggests "reanimation", was derived from a Hebrew chant which Koteliansky sang for Lawrence and Frieda, *Ranane Sadikhim Sadikhim Badanoi*. Lawrence's utopia, whre the righteous might live in joy, thus took its name from Psalm 33, *Rejoice in the Lord, O ye*

righteous. Many of Lawrence's letters to Koteliansky are concerned with Rananim, for Koteliansky, after Lawrence's
"rejection" of Murry, remained one of the very few people
always worthy to become one of the founding pioneers.
Rananim was usually located in one of the more temperate
parts of America, but from time to time, at least in the letters
to Koteliansky (who maintained contact with some influential
people in Russia after the revolution), the new Soviet state
was a possible locus: especially when for one reason or
another Lawrence had taken against America. On 11 May
1917, while the Russian revolution was coming to a head,
he writes: "I keep my belief in Russia intact, until such time
as I am forced to relinquish it: for it is the only country
where I can plant my hopes. America is a stink-pot in my
nostrils, after having been the land of the future for me."

Lawrence's nonconformist upbringing had implanted in
his mind a vivid millenarianism and desire for a New Jerusa-
lem. On 15 May he writes:

> I feel that our chiefest hope for the future is Russia.
> When I think of the young new country there, I love it
> inordinately. It is the place of hope. We must go, sooner or
> a little later . . . We will go to Russia. Send me a Berlitz
> grammar book, I will begin to learn the language — religi-
> ously. And when Farbman comes back, we will scheme —
> and perhaps you will come down here for a few weeks.
> Nuova speranza — la Russie — *Please send me a grammar
> book.*

On 3 July he writes:

> I was glad to hear of Farbman's safe return, and to have
> hopeful news of Russia. Russia seems to me now the positive
> pole of the world's spiritual energy, and America the nega-
> tive pole . . . How can I write for any Russian audience? —
> the contact is not established. How can the current flow
> when there is no connection? As for England, it is quite
> hopeless.

The impulse came to nothing: but in December 1922, he writes from Mexico to Catherine Carswell: "I think I should like to go to Russia in the summer. After America, it appeals to me. No money there (they say). When you write to poor Ivy, ask her how it would be for me and Frieda to spend a few months in Russia — even a year. I feel drawn that way." To Koteliansky, in January 1926, he repeats his wish to learn Russian, along with the faith in the "promised land": "That Rananim of ours, it has sunk out of sight . . . If you will send me a grammar book, I'll begin to learn Russian. Just an ordinary grammar book. Even if I never do go to Russia, it'll do me no harm." He got his grammar: in fact Koteliansky sent him four, and he evidently, for a time at least, put them to good use: "I have bravely started, and am in the midst of those fearful *М* and *ц ц б э* and *ч* things. I hope the bolsheviks, with the end of the Romanovs, ended a few letters of the alphabet. Did they?"[7]

Frieda testifies that "He learnt quite a lot and sat in the evening making Russian noises" (letter of 15 March 1926); but his "influenza" stopped him, and that, it seems, was the end of it. Soon his opinion of the new regime in Russia changed: on 17 May 1926 he tells Koteliansky that the bolsheviks are "loutish and common", seeing them only in terms of disintegration and the triumph of the inorganic, as he had seen Dostoevsky. The plan to communicate with Gorky in connection with the latter's paper *New Life* similarly came to nothing (letter to Koteliansky, 15 May 1917), and the same fate befell the scheme for Koteliansky to translate *Women in Love* into Russian, and arrange for it to be first published in Russia (letter to Koteliansky of 9 February 1917); this was in any case something of a desperate ploy, consequent upon the suppression of *The Rainbow* and its seizure by the police in 1915.

So Russia was to remain for Lawrence a "country of the mind". In this respect Russia played a quite different kind of part in Lawrence's life from the part played by Italy, since, as Cecchetti rather briskly puts it, "Lawrence spent many years of his restless life in Italy, where he hoped to find some of the sound spontaneity of natural instincts for which he was anxiously looking."[8] His first visit, in 1912–13, produced the essays of *Twilight in Italy*, undoubtedly one of his most important works and inextricably linked with both his creative and speculative work in the period. The second visit stretched, with interruptions, from 1919 to 1921. Although it was during this visit that Lawrence worked on Verga, this was not, as Cecchetti asserts, the time of his first "discovering" the Italian author. A letter to Koteliansky, which Cecchetti could not have known (December 1916), contains a reference to Verga's most famous piece: "We have read the *Cavalleria Rusticana*: a veritable blood-pudding of *passion*! It is not at all good, only, in some odd way, comical, as the portentous tragic Italian is always comical." The reservations about "the Italian" are comparable to those in *Twilight in Italy*, but of course the judgement upon Verga represents an initial reaction which Lawrence soon thought better of. If the Italians, as Lawrence believed, are "always acting up to somebody else's vision of life" (essay on *Mastro-Don Gesualdo*), it is from a naivety which is bound up with their essentially true and unselfconscious vision of life:

> Dr. Manente certainly never pitied himself; that is to his credit, vastly: when we think how a modern would howl to the world at large. No, they weren't sorry for themselves — they were tough without being hard-boiled. The courage of life is splendid in them. We badly need some of it today, in this self-pitying age when we are so sorry for ourselves that we have to be soothed by art as by candy. [Preface, *The Story of Dr Manente*]

The "self-pity" that goes with self-consciousness Lawrence attributes to Russians and more especially the "willy wet-leg" Chekhov (letter to Rhys Davies, Christmas Day 1928; I am not suggesting that this is a very intelligent comment). Lawrence does, however, rise above the level of generalised invective and in his *Mastro-Don Gesualdo* esssay does make some suggestive remarks about the peculiarly influential status of Russian literature in the modern period

> Of course your soul will coruscate, if you think it does. That's why the Russians are so popular. No matter how much of a shabby animal you may be, you can learn from Dosteovsky and Chekhov, etc., how to have the most tender, unique, coruscating soul on earth. And so you may be vastly important to yourself. Which is the private aim of all men. The hero had it openly. The commonplace person has it inside himself, though outwardly he says: Of course I'm no better than anybody else! His very asserting it shows he doesn't think it for a second. Every character in Dostoevsky or Chekhov thinks himself inwardly a nonesuch, absolutely unique.

The pressure behind such writing is intensely personal; often when Lawrence writes "Dostoevsky" he means "John Middleton Murry", for Murry wrote an idiosyncratic study of Dostoevsky in 1916 which contributed significantly to that writer's English reputation. In 1915 Lawrence had been reading the Dostoevsky letters, and at that time found him "a great man, and I have the greatest admiration for him", as he told Koteliansky in a letter from May of that year. But by 1916 his opinion had changed: "he has lost his spell over me", he writes in February 1916, and in December of the same year describes Dostoevsky's *Dream of a Queer Fellow*, with an introduction by Murry, as "offal, putrid stuff". The tendency to associate Dostoevsky with Murry by no means abated: near the end of his life, when he seems to have been thinking about Dostoevsky again, he writes to Charles Lahr (14 September 1929) in connection with some plans for editing a satirical journal as follows:

> What one *might* have is a column of imaginary reviews: "Shorter Notices. Life of J. M M. by J. C. This is a work

which cannot be lightly dismissed. The author has gazed into the flowing stream of introspection, and seen, as in a glass, darkly, the great image of — himself etc."

Murry had of course written a life of Christ: this presumably was to have been Christ's revenge, though it is certainly immoderate of Lawrence to continue by referring to Murry under the name of the scapegoat of the Karamazovs: "So there is now Smerdyakov on God! I feel it's about time the Great Dragon swallowed that small fry of treachery. But England will stand by hypocrisy for ever." By this time of course Lawrence was aware of, and resented, Frieda's intimacy with Murry. It is no doubt for reasons connected with this personal pattern of associations, as well as for intrinsic reasons, that Lawrence's comments on Dostoevsky are so often concerned with Dostoevsky's "spirituality", his religious aspect. Lawrence launched an attack on "these self-divided, gamin-religious Russians who are so absorbedly concerned with their own dirty linen and their own piebald souls" with Murry, more than Dostoevsky and Chekhov, in mind. Rozanov he at first thought, as he said, "a pup out of the Dostoevsky kennel"; and in the course of his actually very sympathetic review of Rozanov's *Solitaria*, reprinted in *Phoenix One*, he repeats the same strictures, this time in a kind of grotesque knockabout —

And, of course, in Mary-Mary-quite-contrary we have the ever-recurrent whimper: *I* want to be good! I *am* good: Oh, I am *so* good, I'm better than anybody! I love Jesus and all the saints, and above all, the blessed Virgin! Oh, how I love purity! — and so forth. Then they give a loud crepitus ventris as a punctuation.

In this same essay Lawrence remarks that he is tired of being told that Dostoevsky's *Legend of the Grand Inquisitor* is a profound masterpiece. Yet at the very end of his life, in fact in his last year, in the preface to *The Grand Inquisitor* that he provided for Koteliansky, his opinion has changed, and he is less concerned to evaluate Dostoevsky and more concerned to describe this work in its own terms, accepting its deeper "truth" in the spirit in which he approached American literature in his *Studies in Classic American Literature*:

> It is a strange experience, to examine one's reaction to a book over a period of years. I remember when I first read *The Brothers Karamazov* in 1913, how fascinated yet unconvinced it left me. And I remember Middleton Murry saying to me: 'Of course the whole clue to Dostoevsky is in that Grand Inquisitor story.' And I remember saying: 'Why? It seems to me just rubbish.'
>
> Since then I have read *The Brothers Karamazov* twice, and each time found it more depressing, because, alas, more drearily true to life. At first it had been lurid romance. Now I read *The Grand Inquisitor* once more, and my heart sinks right through my shoes. I still see a trifle of satanical-cynical showing-off. But under that I hear the final and unanswerable criticism of Christ.

But the "truth" of *The Grand Inquisitor* must already have disclosed itself to the Lawrence of the "nightmare" year 1916, since the collapse of individual integrity and responsibility seemed to him to date from that year: so it is very likely that, but for Murry, Lawrence would have written differently about Dostoevsky in earlier years. Already in 1926, three years before the "rediscovery" of Dostoevsky, and the year of his second attempt to learn Russian, he had written to Koteliansky: "I have been thinking lately, the time has come to read Dostoevsky again: not as fiction, but as life. I am so weary of the English way of reading nothing but fiction in everything. I will order *Karamazov* at once."

However, it was not only the vagaries of his relationship with Murry that coloured Lawrence's reading of Dostoevsky: there was in addition an important literary-critical influence on his views. This was the curious quasi-philosophy of Leo

Shestov, a characteristic product of the Russian literary tradition whose work has little in common with anything in English. Shestov's *Apotheosis of Groundlessness*, or *All Things are Possible*, is mentioned by D. J. Gordon in the following terms:

> In the thematic title of Shestov's *All Things are Possible* (for a translation of which he wrote a brief preface in 1920) Lawrence found an echo of one of his own abiding convictions, and he called it, 'when dressed up in a little comely language, a real ideal, that will last us for a new, long epoch.' [. . .] But the book seems to have made no lasting impression on him. He has forgotten it seven years later when, in reviewing Rozanov's *Solitaria* and *The Apocalypse of Our Times*, he praises the author as 'the first Russian . . . who has ever said anything to me.' Rozanov 'is the first to see that immortality is in the vividness of life, not in the loss of life . . . he has more or less recovered the genuine pagan vision, the phallic vision, and with those eyes he looks, in amazement and consternation, on the mess of Christianity . . . Rozanov matters, for the future.

The usefulness of Gordon's allusion to this book is somewhat vitiated by the fact that he does not care to explore its importance beyond the significance of the title (which he seems to think was Shestov's own). Moreover, the publication of the Koteliansky correspondence has made it possible to trace the magnitude of Lawrence's involvement with the book: not only was the work he did as co-translator very considerable, as I shall show, but in addition he wrote his own preface to take the place of Shestov's as a way of providing more effective advocacy for an author he greatly admired.[9] It can also be shown that despite the comments Gordon cites with reference to Rozanov Lawrence had not in fact forgotten Shestov later in the 1920s. If it were literally true, in any case, it would mean that Lawrence had found nothing in the classic Russian novelists, which is evidently without foundation. In fact Lawrence writes to Koteliansky in September 1929 linking the two authors:

> I was thinking, one day we must rescue the Shestov translation from Martin Secker. If the Mandrake have any success with Rozanov, we ought to follow it up with a new edition of *All Things are Possible*. I suppose Secker has let the thing lapse out of print long ago, and no intention of reprinting.

However, there is more interesting evidence of Lawrence's involvement with Shestov. Three letters, in particular, describe the birth-pangs of *All Things are Possible*: all of them, addressed to Koteliansky, date from 1919, and offer a clear evidence of the extent of Lawrence's involvement with this translation.[10]

> I have done a certain amount of the translation — Apotheosis. I began Russian Spirit, but either Shestov writes atrociously — I believe he does — or you translate loosely. One sentence has nothing to do with the next, so that it seems like jargon. The Apotheosis is more intelligible. His attitude amuses me — also his irony, which I think is difficult for English readers. But he isn't anything wonderful, is he? "Apotheosis of Groundlessness" will never do. What can one find instead, for a title?

> I have done 71 of the Shestov paragraphs — more than half. No, I don't hate doing it — rather like it — only he often irritates me when he will keep going on about philosophers, and what they do or don't do. One gets sick of the name of philosophers — But sometimes he blossoms into a kind of pathetic beauty.

> I have finished Shestov — have compressed him a bit, but left nothing out — only 'so to speak' and 'as all know' and many such phrases and volatile sentences — no *substance* at all — sometimes I have added a word or two, for

the sake of the sense — as I did in *Russian Spirit*. What I leave out I leave out deliberately. There is a many-wordedness often, which becomes cloying, wearying — I do get tired of his tilting with "metaphysics", positivism, Kantian postulates, and so on — but I *like* his "flying in the face of Reason" like a cross hen.

It is not surprising that Lawrence should have appended a paragraph on Shestov's style, then, to his preface to *All Things are Possible*, when he had wrestled with it so closely:

> Shestov's style is puzzling at first. Having found the "ands" and "buts" and "becauses" and "therefores" hampered him, he clips them all off deliberately and even spitefully, so his thought is like a man with no buttons on his clothes, ludicrously hitching along all undone. One must be amused, not irritated. Where the armholes were a bit tight, Shestov cuts a slit. It is baffling, but really rather piquant. The real conjunction, the real unification, lies in the reader's own amusement, not in the author's unbroken logic.

— a not altogether different kind of satisfaction from that afforded by many of Lawrence's own critical-speculative works, with their quasi-allegorical devices. Koteliansky objected to Lawrence's preface because he felt, obscurely, that it would damage the cause of Russian literature (this being a period of intense propagandist activity on the part of Russianists).[11] The essence of this short preface is in fact material from Shestov's text extracted by Lawrence and written up by him somewhat, in accordance with his own critical opinions. Thus he takes up Shestov's observations in paragraph 22 of his book (this being its system of organisation) concerning nineteenth-century Russian literature's reaction to the grafting on of an alien western culture (in itself a highly debatable thesis, but one with which Lawrence was predisposed to agree) and renders them more emphatic. This is

Shestov, though in Lawrence's translation (which I shall shortly say more about):

> To us in Russia, civilisation came suddenly, while we were still savages . . . We quickly submitted. In a short time we were swallowing in enormous doses those poisons which Europe had been gradually accustoming herself to, gradually assimilating through centuries . . . A Russian had only to catch a whiff of European atmosphere, and his head began to swim . . .

Lawrence evidently approves of this, and his version of this hypothesis in his preface is consistent with his remarks of five or six years before about the limitations of the classic Russian novel, and his "diagnostic" approach to Russian fiction (as opposed to his warm acceptance of Verga):

> They [i.e. the Russians] have only been inoculated with the virus of European culture and ethic. The virus works in them like a disease . . . Russian art . . . is not spontaneous utterance . . . it is a surgical outcry, horrifying or marvellous, lacerating at first; but when we get used to it, not really so profound, not really ultimate, a little extraneous.[12]

Lawrence, in other words, has found an authentic Russian authority to strengthen and support his unfashionably negative attitude to Russian literature. And in Lawrence's translation, the terms in which Shestov continues his argument have a remarkably Lawrentian ring:

> Well, and what does all the "finish" and the completeness signify? It merely means that none of our western neighbours will end his speech before the last reassuring word is said; he will never let nature have the last word; so he rounds off his synthesis . . . Thus there lies before us the choice between the artistic and accomplished lie of old, cultured Europe, a lie which is the outcome of a thousand

years of hard and bitter effort, and the artless, sincere simplicity of young, uncultured Russia.

"Two bodies of modern literature have come to a real verge: the Russian and the American." Even the brutal and mechanical clean sweep of bolshevism could at times impress Lawrence, if it flowered in the new truth lying dormant in "young uncultured Russia", "the young new country", for, as he said, "Russia seems to me now the positive pole of the world's spiritual energy." Shestov powerfully reinforced certain existing structural oppositions in Lawrence's peculiar psychic geography; but in addition, some of Lawrence's more specific critical observations on Tolstoy, Dostoevsky, and more deviously Chekhov, are supported by Shestov and may very well originate with him (though as I shall show there is a slight element of distortion). Lawrence, for example, did not accept what Murry saw as the "message" of Dostoevsky, a new gospel of Christian love. In the *Grand Inquisitor* preface he describes Dostoevsky as "always perverse, always impure, always an evil thinker and a marvellous seer", and in the essay on Rozanov's *Solitaria* he writes: "For the first time we get what we have got from no Russian, neither Tolstoi nor Dostoevsky nor any of them, a real, positive view on life." Both of these observations could be traced back to Shestov's thirty-third paragraph (headed significantly "Dostoevsky — advocatus diaboli"), in which we find the following section:

> Dostoevsky attacked Lutheranism, and pitied the old catholicism and the breathless heights to which its "spiritual" children had risen. Wholesome morality and its support is not enough for Dostoevsky. All this is not "positive", it is only "protest". Whether I am believed or not, I will repeat that Vladimir Soloviov, who held that Dostoevsky was a prophet, is wrong, and that N. K. Mikhailovsky, who calls him a cruel talent and a grubber after buried treasure, is right. Dostoevsky grubs after buried treasure — no doubt about that. And, therefore, it would be

more becoming in the younger generation that still marches
under the flag of pious idealism if, instead of choosing
him as a spiritual leader, they avoided the old sorceror, in
whom only those gifted with great short-sightedness or
lack of experience in life could fail to see the dangerous
man.

But by juxtaposing this passage with Lawrence's own comments on Dostoevsky (particularly with the more hostile
judgements in the *Letters, passim*) we should not make the
mistake of supposing that Shestov is evaluating Dostoevsky
along Lawrentian lines. Some ambiguities in the passage I
have cited furnish a clue to a slight distortion of Shestov's
text in Lawrence's translation. There is no doubt that the
Russian critic was fighting a running battle with the forces
of idealism, as Lawrence was, but it was important for him to
instruct the younger generation of Russian writers in a true
reading of Dostoevsky, that is, one that did not throw the
emphasis on to the overt "message" or "content" of what
Bakhtin has called "polyphonic" texts.[13] Lawrence has, for
instance, misread the Mikhailovsky allusion as an adverse
value-judgement, instead of a characteristically paradoxical
but at a deeper level objective remark about the nature (and
supreme importance) of Dostoevsky's genius: and the misreading involves an act of mistranslation, for the Russian
phrase which he renders "Dostoevsky grubs after buried
treasure" is in the original "Dostoevsky iskal kladov", where
the verb means simply "sought". Shestov means surely that
Dostoevsky dug deep in order to seek out hidden sources of
character and action, and should be read with a comparable
attentiveness to what is "hidden": whereas, by his use of the
word "grubs", Lawrence associates Dostoevsky, as elsewhere,
with predatory rodents and insects. So that if Lawrence was
"influenced" here by Shestov, he has not given proper weight
to the irony or ambivalence in Shestov's tone, despite the
fact that he drew attention to it in his letters while working
on the translation. When Shestov called Dostoevsky "opasny

chelovek", "a dangerous man", he had something different
in mind from Lawrence's repugnance for the author described
by Murry in his study as: "A prophet . . . . who contemplated
and sought to penetrate into a new consciousness and a new
mode of being which he saw was metaphysically inevitable
for mankind."[14] And concomitantly, where Shestov makes
value-judgements which are unequivocally positive (which is
not often), Lawrence dilutes the praise:

> . . . а в *Записках из Подполья* и остальных своих
> произведениях он умнейший и проницательнейший человек.

> . . . but in his *Letters from the Underworld* and the rest of
> his books he is the shrewdest and cleverest of writers.

Lawrence says "shrewdest and cleverest" where Shestov has
"wisest and most penetrating", and by doing so attributes to
Dostoevsky qualities which, from experience of Lawrence's
work, one would judge to be less than supremely admirable.
Working from Koteliansky's draft, of course, Lawrence
would have been able to shelter behind his ignorance of the
Russian text: but in fact he seems to have been aware of the
liberty he was taking, and to have chosen his words with care.
   I would not claim that Lawrence needed Shestov to justify
his evaluation of Dostoevsky: there are letters from 1915 and
1916, in any case, which comment on Dostoevsky in Shestovian terms before, presumably, Lawrence had read Shestov's
book. But it is nevertheless interesting that certain Shestovian
formulations stayed with Lawrence, doubtless as a consequence of his close linguistic involvement in the translation
process. This can be seen even more clearly in the case of
Tolstoy and Chekhov. Lawrence's hostility to Tolstoy's
moral scheme in *Anna Karenina* has often caused puzzlement,
at least in the Anglo-Saxon world, where Tolstoy had been
read, on the whole, through Victorian spectacles as a kind of
Russian George Eliot. Most often cited in this regard is a passage in which Lawrence defies "old Leo", a passage which

Leavis, for instance, finds "astonishing":

> Nobody in the world is anything but delighted when
> Vronsky gets Anna Karenina. Then what about the sin?
> Why, when you look at it, all the tragedy comes from
> Vronsky's and Anna's fear of society. The monster was
> social, not phallic at all. They couldn't live in the pride
> of their sincere passion, and spit in Mother Gundy's eye.
> And that, that cowardice, was the real "sin". The novel
> makes it obvious, and knocks all old Leo's teeth out.

Leavis comments in his well-known essay on *Anna Karenina*[15]
that, "It is astonishing that so marvellously perceptive a critic
as Lawrence could simplify in that way, with so distorting an
effect." He finds a suggestive parallel in Lawrence's own life,
and in Frieda, as Lawrence tells us on one occasion, reading
Anna Karenina in a "how to be happy though livanted"
spirit. But although Lawrence's tone, especially in the *Reflections on the Death of a Porcupine* essay, is immoderate, the
kind of reading he gives the book (i.e. *against* the author) is
consistent with his approach to literature elsewhere, and the
specific judgement he makes on its moral standpoint is not
merely personal: at all events, it squares with Shestov, who is
well aware of the perverse strain in Tolstoy:

> Para 78. Young, inexperienced writers usually believe in
> harmonia praestabilitata, even though they have never
> heard of Leibnitz . . . Tolstoy now believed, and now dis-
> believed, according to the work he had in hand. When he
> had other people's ideas to destroy he doubted the identity
> of egoistic and idealist aspirations; when he had his own to
> defend, he believed in it. Which is a line of conduct worthy
> of imitation; for human truths are proper exclusively for
> ancillary purposes . . .

> Para 80. When he was young, Tolstoy wanted to make men
> happy; when he was old, he knew he could not make them

happy, he began to preach renunciation, resignation, and so forth. And how angry he got when people wouldn't have his teaching!

Para 96. How can the morality of Tolstoy's heroes be trusted? Consciousness of one's ugliness begets shyness, shyness drives the passions inwards and allows them no natural outlet [Shestov is referring specifically to Nickolenka in *Childhood*]. Little by little there develops a monstrous discrepancy between the imagination and its desires, on the one hand, and the power to satisfy these desires, on the other. Permanent hunger, and a contracted alimentary canal, which does not pass the food through. Hence the hatred of the imagination, with its unrealised and unrealisable cravings . . . In our day no one has scourged love so cruelly as Tolstoy in *Power of Darkness*. But the feats of the village Don Juan need not necessarily end in tragedy. "More than anything on earth", however, Tolstoy hates the Don Juans, the handsome, brave, successful, the self-confident, who spontaneously act upon suggestion, the conquerors of women, who stretch out their hands to living statues cold as stone. As far as ever he can he has his revenge on them in his writing.

Part Two Para 3. In Tolstoy's view morality grows stronger the harder the job it has to tackle. It pardons the weak offenders without waste of words, but it never forgives pride and self-confidence. If Tolstoy's edicts had been executed, all memorials to Poushkin would have disappeared; chiefly because of the poet's addiction to the eternal female. In such a case Tolstoy is implacable. He admits the kind of love whose object is the establishing of a family, but no more. Don Juan is a hateful transgressor. Think of Levin, and his attitude to prostitutes. He is exasperated, indignant, even forgets the need for compassion, and calls them "beasts". In the eternal female Tolstoy sees temptation, seduction, sin, *great danger*. Therefore it is necessary to keep quite away from the danger. But surely danger is the dragon which guards every treasure on earth. And again, no matter what his precautions, a man will meet his fate sooner or later, and come into conflict with the dragon. Surely this is an axiom . . . Tolstoy was the first among us . . . who began to fear life. He was the first to start open moralising . . . Tolstoy preserved himself on account of his inborn instinct for departing betimes from a dangerous situation.

If the length of the quotations is excessive, my justification is the scarcity of the text. At this point I ought to add that Lawrence has not significantly altered the Russian in the process of translating.

Evidently, a number of critical attitudes here are echoed in Lawrence's comments on Tolstoy. Where Shestov speaks of an "identity of egoistic and idealistic aspirations", Lawrence, calling Tolstoy a "child of Law", says he had a "marvellous sensuous understanding and very little clarity of mind". Lawrence's scepticism about the basis of Tolstoy's moral authority, his express opinion that it sprang from a sense of inadequacy, or age, is close to Shestov, who, in finding fault with the harsh moralist in Tolstoy, expresses a view which has plenty of support in Tolstoy's own comments on his work in later life. For some reason English critics have paid little attention to the contradictions in Tolstoy's life and art, and have accepted his moral authoritarianism with fewer qualms than Tolstoy himself reveals in connection with it. Lawrence's comments, though they are delivered in a tone which, even for him, is off-hand, are not in themselves so puzzling.

By way of concluding this consideration of Lawrence and Shestov, which could of course be extended far beyond the limits of the present discussion, it is worth noting that Lawrence's unfashionable impatience with Chekhov apparently derives support from Shestov: I say "apparently" because once again there is some element of distortion in the translation, although it is quite clear that Shestov's ironical Chek-

hov, mirrored by Lawrence, is a different proposition from
the narcissistic poet of the twilight admired by the English
Chekhovians. The following passage is representative:

> Дядя Ваня, 5о-легный старик, не своим голосом кричит на всю
> сцену, на весь мир: "пропала жизнь, пропала хизнь", и
> безсмысленно стрелает в ничем неповинного профессора.

Uncle Vanya, an old man of fifty, cries beside himself all
over the stage, "My life is done for, my life is done for",
and senselessly shoots at a harmless professor.

The belittling effect of "all over the stage" and "harmless" is
clear enough, and "my life is done for", as well as being
somewhat unnatural as a phrase, does not quite correspond
to "propala zhizn". Lawrence is mocking Chekhov; Shestov
was underlining and interpreting the absurd element (by no
means simply the ridiculous) in his characters. For purposes
of comparison it is interesting to look at Shestov's French
translator, the distinguished Russianist Boris de Schloezer, who
rendered with a strikingly different objectivity and accuracy
a longer account of *Uncle Vanya* that Lawrence could be
accused of enlisting in his own ends:

> Vania sent que le docteur éprouve la même soif de consola-
> tion. Et la pauvre Sonia n'a pas la force, elle non plus, de
> supporter sa peine de jeune fille solitaire. Les yeux épou-
> vantés, hagards, ils cherchent tous un homme capable de les
> décharger d'une partie au moins de leur insupportable tour-
> ment, mais la situation est la même pour tous. Ils sont tous
> trop lourdement chargés, aucun d'eux n'a la force de
> supporter ses propres maux, et il ne peut être question
> pour eux de se charger encore des peines d'autrui. L'auteur
> enlève à ces malheureux la dernière consolation qui leur re-
> stait: ils ne peuvent se plaindre, ils ne rencontrent nulle
> pitié; l'angoisse et le désespoir sont inscrits sur tous les visages
> qui les entourent. Chacun doit porter sa croix et se taire.
> Personne ne pleure et ne prononce de paroles attendrissantes;

cela serait inconvenant et déplacé. Quand l'oncle Vania qui ne s'était pas immédiatement rendu compte que sa situation était sans issue, se met à crier, "Ma vie est ratée!" personne ne prête attention à ses clameurs. "Elle est ratée! Et puis après! Tout le monde le sait bien! Tais-toi! Les cris n'y feront rien!

And in the more vivid but, as I have verified, less accurate version by Lawrence and Koteliansky:

Vanya finds that the doctor himself has an unquenchable thirst for consolation and encouragement, whilst poor Sonya can bear her maiden sorrows no longer. They all go wandering round with big, lost eyes, looking for someone to relieve them from *part* of their woes, at least. And lo, everybody is in the same street as themselves. All are over-heavy-laden, not one can carry his own burden, let alone give a lift to another's. The last consolation is taken away. It is no use complaining: there is no sympathetic response. On all faces the same expression of hopelessness and despair. Each must bear his cross in silence. None may weep or utter pitiful cries — it would be uncalled-for and indecent. When Uncle Vanya, who has not realised at once the extremity of his situation, begins to cry out: "My life's a waste!" nobody wants to listen to him. "Waste, waste! Everybody knows it's a waste! Shut your mouth, howling won't help you."

The force of such loaded phrases in the translation as "maiden sorrows" or "they all go wandering round" or "all are over-heavy-laden" is to express critical dissent from both Shestov and Chekhov; it seems to be the voice of Lawrence that shouts "howling won't help you". Unresponsive to Shestov's irony, despite his remarks upon it, and equally unresponsive to Chekhov's, Lawrence, as we know, wrote off Chekhov, crudely, as a "willy wet-leg": an odd phrase to characterise an exceptionally courageous writer. But of course the target was no so much Chekhov as the English Chekhovians: and in this respect Lawrence's invective was not altogether unmotivated, since, at the very least, they can be accused of misinterpreting Chekhov.

Lawrence was writing his "pollyanalytics", his "philosophy" (he used both terms somewhat ironically) when he read Shestov: it is known now as the *Study of Thomas Hardy*, and is one of his best speculative pieces. A number of passages from *All Things are Possible* may be set alongside Lawrence's text to reveal a kinship in respect of general moral positions, although the dates of the two works (the Hardy study probably precedes the actual translation work on Shestov by a few years) make direct influence unlikely, and perhaps both authors are responding to a common influence, probably Nietzsche:

> Para 120. Morality, which lays down definite rules and thereby guards life for a time from any surprise, exists only by convention, and in the end collapses before the non-moral surging-up of individual human aspirations. Laws — all of them — have only a regulating value, and are necessary only to those who want rest and security. But the first and essential condition of life is lawlessness. Laws are a refreshing sleep — lawlessness is creative activity.

There is an apparent similarity between this and the following passage from the *Study*:

> Upon the vast, incomprehensible pattern of some primal morality greater than ever the human mind can grasp, is drawn the little, pathetic pattern of man's moral life and struggle, pathetic, almost ridiculous. The little fold of law and order, the little walled city within which man has to defend himself from the waste enormity of nature, becomes too small, and the pioneers venturing out with the code of the walled city upon them, die in the bonds of that code, free and yet unfree, preaching the walled city and looking to the waste.

Occasionally we come upon a passage in *All Things are Possible* where Lawrence's style, as translator, has left such an indelible mark that we seem to be reading a page of one of his own essays:

> Para 32. Even we go so far as to assert that had we the power we would change nothing, absolutely nothing in the world. An' yet, if by some miracle such power came into our hands, how triumphantly we would send to the devil all philosophies and lofty world-conceptions, all ideals and metaphysics, and plainly and simply, without reflection, abolish sufferings, deformities, failures, all those things to which we attach such a high educational value, abolish them from the face of the earth. We are fed up, oh, how fed up we are with carrying on our studies. But it can't be helped. Faute de mieux, let us keep on inventing systems, thinking them out. But let us agree not to be cross with those who don't want to have anything to do with our system. Really, they have a perfect right.

As a matter of fact the tone here, even of those characteristically Lawrentian expostulations ("oh, how fed up we are") exactly renders the original. The combination of a speculative "metaphysics", utopianism, and pragmatism here is close to Lawrence's own manner. To such an extent, at any rate, was Shestov a kindred spirit, and Gordon was surely mistaken to dismiss him so summarily, for *All Things are Possible* is relevant to the important topic of Lawrence's relationship with the Russian literary tradition. When Lawrence came to read Rozanov's *Solitaria* and *Fallen Leaves* at the end of his life, his delight in finding an author who was Russian yet not "a pup out of the Dostoevsky kennel" is consistent with the evaluation of Dostoevsky's work he found, or thought he found, in Shestov: and it was at this point that he expressed his wish to get *All Things are Possible* back into print. Rozanov "matters, for the future" because he charts a course away from the "mess of Christianity" towards "the genuine pagan vision". The "tortured complexity of Christian civilisation" which was Dostoevsky's legacy, and in a different way Tolstoy's too, was rejected by the Nietzschean Rozanov. This is doubtless why the author of *The Plumed Serpent* and *Lady Chatterley's Lover* greeted Rozanov as "the first Russian . . . who has ever said anything to me". Rozanov in fact served rather as the ultimate stage of the thought-adventure pursued by Lawrence among Russian authors. He represents one side of a dialectic of which the other, contrary thesis is that signified by Italy and in particular the work of Giovanni Verga.

NOTES

1. D. J. Gordon, *D. H. Lawrence as a Literary Critic* (New Haven and London: Yale UP, 1966).
2. These antithetical terms are drawn from Lawrence's own *Study of Thomas Hardy* reprinted in *Phoenix One*. Cf. J. N. R. Saunders, *D. H. Lawrence and Italy*, unpublished B. Phil. thesis.
3. Harry T. Moore (ed.), *The Collected Letters of D. H. Lawrence*, p. 469.
4. This extract forms part of a much longer argument.
5. *Phoenix One*, 1936.
6. George J. Zytaruk, *The Quest for Rananim*.
7. Transcribed from Lawrence's manuscript.
8. Giovanni Cecchetti, 'Verga and D. H. Lawrence's Translations', *Comparative Literature*.
9. Cf. George J. Zytaruk, op. cit.
10. These letters, from the Koteliansky papers, are included in George J. Zytaruk's *The Quest for Rananim*, op. cit.
11. George J. Zytaruk and other scholars have drawn attention to the extraordinary proliferation of generally high quality translations of Russian literature in the first twenty years of this century.
12. If we disallow the value-judgement here, it is nevertheless worth noting that writers from within the Russian tradition, like Solzhenitsyn, have commented on the "extraneous" nature of western philosophy in Russian literature.
13. Mikhail Bakhtin, *Problems of Dostoevsky's Poetics* (Ann Arbor: Ardis, 1973).
14. J. M. Murry, *Fyodor Dostoevsky* (London: Cape, 1916).
15. F. R. Leavis, *Anna Karenina and Other Essays*, (London: Chatto & Windus, 1967).

2 Lawrence and Verga: The Short Stories

Lawrence published three volumes of translations from Verga: the novel *Mastro-Don Gesualdo* (Seltzer, 1923), *Little Novels of Sicily* (Seltzer, 1925), and *Cavalleria Rusticana* (Cape, 1928). In disregard of chronology, I wish to discuss the short stories first, since it is only with these that the long essay by Cecchetti to which I have already referred is concerned, and this essay raises a number of points of general interest in the discussion of the whole body of Lawrence's translations from the Italian.

Verga is one of the greatest of modern Italian prose writers, with a secure classic status. J. H. Whitfield, in his *Short History of Italian Literature*, calls him "the most substantial of the Italian veristi";[1] but the interesting point here (and the one which clearly attracted Lawrence, as he says practically in so many words) was that Verga made a sudden volte-face, and turned away from his earlier, French mode of realism in favour of the peasant subjects of his mature work, which is concerned almost entirely with a primitive Sicilian community. In his own dismissive words, he characterised his early work as "falso nell'arte com'ero fuori del vero nella vita" — a judgement which links his life and his art, saying that *he* (the artist) was as false in his art as he was remote from the truth in his living: a linking of art to life which one might expect to appeal to Lawrence. These false works are such novels as *Eva* and *Eros*, on which his early reputation was founded, and of which Lawrence says in his preface to *Cavalleria Rusticana*:

They are interesting, alive, bitter, somewhat unhealthy, smelling of the seventies and of the Paris of the Goncourts, and in some curious way abortive. The man had not found himself. He was in his wrong element, fooling himself and being fooled by show, in a true Italian fashion.

And it seemed to Lawrence, even when he had developed the highest regard for Verga, that he had still a legacy of false "Frenchy" ideas about writing, the most misleading and erroneous of them being the idea of self-effacement:

Verga was caught up by the grand idea of self-effacement in art. Anything more confused, more silly, really, than the pages prefacing the excellent story "Gramigna's Lover" would be hard to find, from the pen of a great writer . . . The theories were none of his own, just borrowed from the literary smarties of Paris.

Lawrence goes on to say that self-effacement of this kind is nothing but a form of self-consciousness, that self-consciousness which had taken a more evidently introverted form in Russian fiction and was now threatening the "Homeric" objectivity of Verga's world, a world where, in Lawrentian terms, Law was more powerful than Love. Evidently Lawrence wants Verga to out-Verga himself: in point of fact the sophisticated writer, a category which includes both Lawrence and Verga, is always an intruder in any "primitive" world he may call into being, as both authors recognise in their different ways. Nevertheless it *is* a shock when, after half a dozen stories in the *Cavalleria Rusticana* collection, when we have entered with remarkable completeness into the subtle but unconscious, law-bound moral world of Verga's Sicily, the author intrudes with a kind of nervous insouciance, dressed, as Lawrence neatly puts it, in his "Paris ready-mades":

Dear Farina, I'm sending you here not a story but the outlines of a story . . . I believe that the triumph of the novel, that most complete and most human of all works of art, will be reached when the affinity and the cohesion of all its parts will be so complete that the process of the creation will remain a mystery, a mystery as great as that of the development of the human passions; and that the harmony of its form will be so perfect, the sincerity of its content so evident, its method and its raison d'être so necessary, that the hand of the artist will remain absolutely invisible.

This sounds more like Joyce than like Lawrence, whose improvisatory novels of the 1920s were "unfinished" and closely bound up with the imaginative life of their author. Erroneous doctrines of impersonality are associated by Lawrence with Verga's occasional pedantic deliberateness ("we need more looseness"), and there is some justice in Lawrence's judgement. Yet for all that, "Verga's people are always people in the purest sense of the word . . . What Verga's soul yearned for was the purely naive human being, in contrast to the sophisticated."[2] "Yearned" is appropriate: Lawrence recognises in the Verga simplicity an element of the same deeply felt need that he, too, experienced. And with this image of a type of humanity perhaps, as yet, unborn, goes Lawrence's fascination with Verga's synthetic yet beautifully natural "art-speech", his perfectly wrought Sicilian Italian. Two letters from 1921 make it clear that Lawrence saw Verga's language as a challenge to the translator, and that his wish to translate him was to a large extent an eagerness to take on the challenge: he writes to Catherine Carswell, for example, on 25 October 1921: "Do you know if he is translated into English? *I Malavoglia* or *Mastro-Don Gesualdo*? — or *Novelle Rusticane*, or the other short stories. It would be fun to do him — his *language* is so fascinating." And to Edward Garnett (10 November 1921):

He is extraordinarily good — peasant — quite modern — Homeric — and it would need somebody who could absolutely handle English in the dialect to translate him. He would be most awfully difficult to translate. That is what tempts me: though it is rather a waste of time, and probably I shall never do it. Though if I don't I doubt if anyone else will — adequately, at least.

There is no evidence that Lawrence knew about the existing translations of the short stories, a volume translated by Alma Strattel (London: Pseudonym Library, 1893) and another by Nathan H. Dole (Boston: Joseph Knight, 1898) — doubtless these are not the only ones — though he did at least know of the existence, if no more, of Mary Craig's translations of *I Malavoglia* and *Mastro-Don Gesualdo* (New York: Harper & Row), from 1890 and 1893 respectively, as we know from his letter to Curtis Brown of January 1922. In any case he was sure that no other writer was capable of rising to the challenge of Verga's language, and of creating in English an "art-speech", to use his own term, adequate for the purpose: an idiom, that is, rooted in dialect as Verga's Italian was rooted in Sicilian peasant speech, but without being in any literal sense a transcript of any actual dialect: verisimilitude was not the real point of the exercise, and Verga's language is an artistic synthesis, as is Lawrence's use of dialect even at its most marked, for instance in *Lady Chatterley's Lover*. One of the most interesting and valuable contributions to Harry T. Moore's *A D. H. Lawrence Miscellany* (London: Heinemann, 1961) is that of Elizabeth Mayer, entitled disarmingly 'An Afternoon with D. H. Lawrence', part of which is concerned with just this problem, which evidently fascinated Lawrence and was close to his main preoccupations as an artist with the Letter and the Flesh and the Spirit. Miss Mayer was herself a translator working in German, and when the conversation turned to the subject of translation Lawrence advised her to translate Verga into German. This was in September 1927: she records that Lawrence, who had already translated the *Little Novels of Sicily* and *Mastro-Don Gesualdo*, was working on his *Cavalleria Rusticana* translations. "We had a lively conversation," she recalls, "on the trials of a translator, particularly on the difficulty of translating dialect." Regretting that she had not made an exact transcript of what Lawrence said, she goes on:

> Roughly, Lawrence said that the major problem in handling dialect is how to avoid the two over-simple and absolutely wrong solutions: the first, to translate the dialect of the original into another dialect which is spoken in a geographically existent region (in my case it was Germany) and in a particular locality. For example, one must never have Sicilian peasants express themselves in the equivalent German or Austrian country idiom. Every dialect has inevitable overtones of the landscape, the character of the people and their native customs, inherent in their special locality and radically different from another and foreign region. Morals and manners, valid in Sicilian terms, would seem absurd when twisted into the sounds of a German way of life. On the other hand, it would be just as wrong to transplant the real Sicilian, together with his native peculiarities, into the German-speaking ambiance — simply verbally to reproduce his dialect: it would not ring true at all. Lawrence's advice, therefore, was to avoid both cheap solutions and try to *invent* a new dialect, coined in German words but free from any reference, from any flavour of a special region, yet preserving the flavour of some sort of relaxed, uncitified, untutored mode of speaking. Of course, he did *not* suggest an artificial or synthetic dialect. In his *Little Novels of Sicily* he has certainly solved this problem remarkably, and, with his imaginative insight, has caught the tone of a dialect and so has preserved the freshness of the original.

In this context it is very helpful to have the testimony of a native speaker of Italian, and worth transcribing at length Cecchetti's remarks about Verga's language:[3]

Verga adopted a language that was bare and essential, devoid of all the sensuous ornaments that had previously marked his writings. He rejected the old and new 'literary' ways of expression and resorted to a stylistic technique which, in his opinion, enabled him to reproduce the speech of his people with an almost absolute directness. His syntax acquired an extremely simple appearance; his sentences became sequences of coordinate clauses connected by 'e' or 'che' (frequently a transcription of the Sicilian 'ca') and sometimes became long and rambling. His vocabulary became very popular and so scant that it may be considered one of the most limited in all Italian literature . . . Lawrence felt the regional linguistic stratum lying just beneath the surface of Verga's prose. However, he did not explain how the 'dialect' should be used. Very probably he meant to employ it directly. In parts of the dialogue of *Cavalleria Rusticana* and some other stories (but very inconsistently) he drew from the cockney of London; and there he was in error, because Turiddù, Alfio, Lola, and Santa speak Italian, except for two instances when they speak straight Sicilian. It is true that their Italian is flavored with local color, that sometimes it sounds translated — and indeed it is — but nevertheless it is Italian.

The value of Cecchetti's remarks is unfortunately diminished by a degree of misrepresentation, as well as some assumptions about language which are questionable. He seems, for example, to share those normative assumptions which prompt Italians, sometimes, to maintain that their language is spoken correctly only in Tuscany — "their Italian is flavoured . . . but nevertheless it is Italian." Lawrence's English is English, but neither Lawrence nor Verga are involved in "flavouring" their language with regionalisms, least of all, in Lawrence's case, with what Cecchetti very oddly calls "the cockney of London". Lawrence's use of what is in fact the Nottingham dialect of which he had, it seems, a perfect command, may be illustrated by means of a brief quotation from *Cavalleria Rusticana*: apparently this is what Cecchetti thought was "cockney":

> "It's rare to set eyes on you!" he said to her.
> "Hello, Turiddù! They told me you'd come back on the first of the month."
> "They told me more than that!" he replied. "Is it right as you're marrying Alfio, as contracts for carting?"
> "God willing, I am," replied Lola, twisting the corners of her kerchief at her chin.
> "There's a lot o' God willing about it! You suit your own fancy! And it was God willing as I should come home from as far as I did, to hear this nice bit of news, was it, Lola?"

Or again:

> "Why don't you go and say all those sweet nothings to Mrs. Lola, over the road?" Santa replied to him.
> "Mrs. Lola thinks she's somebody. Mrs. Lola's married My Lord Tom-Noddy, she has."
> "And I'm not good enough for a Lord Tom-Noddy, am I?"
> "You're worth twenty Lolas. And I know somebody as wouldn't look at Mrs. Lola, nor at the saint she's named after, if you was by. Mrs Lola's not fit to bring you your shoes, she's not."

Lawrence uses this idiom extensively in this second collection, which is one reason why it is more interesting and ultimately more satisfying than the earlier collection.[4] The naturalness of this manner, free from any hint of translatorese, is equalled only by its fidelity: a striking fidelity to the letter of Verga's text, and a deeper truth to its emotional organisation. The original Italian of these two passages is as follows:

> —Beato chi vi vede! le disse.
> —Oh, compare Turiddù, me l'avevano detto che siete tornato al primo del mese.

—A me hanno detto dell'altre cose ancora! rispose lui. Che
è vero che vi maritate con compare Alfio, il carrettiere?
—Se c'è la volontà di Dio! rispose Lola tirandosi sul mento
le due cocche del fazzoletto.
—Le volontà di Dio la fate col tira e molla come vi torna
conto! E la volontà di Dio fu che dovevo tornare da tanto
lontano per trovare ste belle notizie, gnà Lola!

and:

> —Perchè non andate a dirle alla gnà Lola ste belle cose?
> rispondeva Santa.
> —La gnà Lola è una signorina! La gnà Lola ha sposato un re
> di corona, ora!
> —Io non me li merito i re di corona.
> —Voi ne valete cento delle Lole, e conosco uno che non
> guarderebbe la gnà Lola, nè il suo santo, quando ci siete
> voi, chè la gnà Lola, non e degna di portarvi le scarpe, non
> è degna.

That very "che" construction which Cecchetti recognises as
Sicilian is employed here ("Che è vero che") so that, even to
a reader whose Italian is not perfect, a dialectal note comes
through, as it does in the idioms and in the fairly numerous
contractions, to all of which Lawrence responds in one way
or another. The phrase "La volontà di Dio la fate col tira e
molla", as well as employing a slightly odd word order, rings
a change on the expression "fare a tira e molla", the dictionary
definition of which is "to shilly-shally", and thus to talk
around something, or not to the point. The effect of this
idiom is surely well caught by Lawrence. Similarly with the
inversion at the beginning of the next sentence, where Lawrence puts in a Nottingham "as" to match Verga's Sicilian
"che". In the second extract, "all those sweet nothings"
serves well as an equivalent for "ste belle cose", with the col-
loquial elision of "queste", while "thinks she's somebody"
brings out the irony underlying "è una signorina". The most
striking colloquialism, "my Lord Tom-Noddy", has pretty

much the same tone as "crowned king" as Verga uses the phrase ("re di corona") in this context. "His sentences sometimes become long and rambling", says Cecchetti of Verga, as if this were an absolute fault of style. Lawrence follows the contours of Verga's loosely articulated periods quite faithfully, with a consequent sense of spontaneity. It is this improvisatory style, perhaps, that prompts Cecchetti to condemn Lawrence on grounds of carelessness. His translations, he says,

> are the enthusiastic work of a man of genius, who did not, or could not, go beyond a first draft. There is no doubt that they would have had great beauty and might even have become works of art in their own right — as is sometimes the case with the translations — if they had been carefully corrected and polished.

Lawrence once remarked bitterly in a letter to Russell that he was always being told, patronisingly, that he was a genius: and Cecchetti's comments go on to make it clear that, for him at least, genius does not compensate for Lawrence's presumptuousness and stylistic viciousness:

> Usually Lawrence translates word for word, adhering more closely to the letter of the text than was wise. Following the original as closely as possible, he translated also Verga's images and idioms, often creating new and very uncommon images in English and achieving the color that British and American reviewers noted in his versions. To create new and uncommon images is the privilege of writers, and the duty of translators when the images are new in the original. However, though aesthetically Verga's images are always new, for they reflect a truly original imagination in their freshness and intensity, linguistically they are not. Lawrence relied far too much on the dictionary.

The last remark seems something of a *non sequitur*, but the point about the way Lawrence has translated Verga's idioms is more significant. Evidently this was not dictated by the exigencies of commerce, as Cecchetti at one point suggests, and the desire to get the work done as quickly as possible; nor by ignorance of the Italian language, even though at certain points this may be arguable. It is, on the contrary, fully consistent with Lawrence's sense of the "spirit of place" and the "otherness" of a distinctive foreign culture which the translator must not lose. Hence a technique of what might be called, in the terminology of Victor Shklovsky, "making strange" or "defamiliarisation".[5] Verga was himself very well aware of this problem, and discussed it with his French translator, Edouard Rod:

> So bene la grande difficoltà che vi e a tradurre in un'altra lingua questi schizzi (*Vita dei Campi*) che hanno una fisonomia tutta loro anche nell'italiano.

> I know well how very difficult it is for you to translate into another language these sketches which even in Italian have distinguishing features all their own.

Verga insists that, at all costs, the peculiarities must not be ironed out, the "fisonomia" or local colour of the language must be preserved: to translate *Mastro-Don Gesualdo* into French is hard:

> e, lo riconosco, di una difficoltà enorme a rendere in un'altra lingua col colore e la fisonomia propria. Pero in questo, solo in questo sta il qualsiasi merito del romanzo e la sua ragione di essere come opera d'arte.

> I know how enormously difficult it is to convey its colour and distinctive features in another language. But whatever merit the novel may have, its raison d'être as a work of art, depends on that, and that alone.[6]

Those few lines I have quoted from *Cavalleria Rusticana*

have, to my mind, the right kind of "fisonomia": they have acquired, partly from associations from Lawrence's own work, an English "fisonomia" which connotes the right kind of remoteness and strangeness, from the standpoint of metropolitan culture. This is an effect of style, since it requires a certain deflection of English away from familiar modes and habits. As in other translations by great writers, the transplanted growth sprouts new roots and puts out new leaves, while remaining recognisably itself, and the translation process seems to continue before one's eyes. The same passage in Cecchetti's translation may serve the purpose of clinching this point:

> "It's a lucky person who sees you!" he said.
> "Oh, Turiddù, they'd told me you came back the first of the month."
> "They told me things too," he answered. "Is it true you're going to marry Alfio, the cart driver?"
> "If that's the will of God!" answered Lola, pulling the two corners of her kerchief over her chin.
> "You make the will of God yourself, just as it happens to suit you! And the will of God was that I should come home from so far away to heat this fine piece of news, Lola."

Cecchetti's Italian is native, Lawrence's is not, but he does not seem, on the evidence of his English, very alert to Verga's rhythms in this masterly dialogue. At one point in his extensive correspondence with Rod, Verga comments in despair on a translation of *Mastro-Don Gesualdo* made by another French translator, on which he was trying to persuade Rod to do a salvage operation:

> La traduttrice non conosca affato l'indole e il valore dell'italiano non solo, ma quasi direi che conosca poco anche il francese.

> The translator not only does not really understand the true character, the value of each word, in the Italian, but I

almost want to say that she does not know French very well, either.

On both these counts Lawrence seems to me better than Cecchetti will allow. With his sensitivity to the "spirit of place" he was intensely, perhaps exaggeratedly, alert to what he saw as the native genius of Italian as a language.[7] But he also had the kind of command of English that is rarely found outside the work of a writer. Verga found the French version of his novel distressingly unidiomatic:

> La mia povera prosa poi — difettosa, tormentosa e tormentata, sia pure, per voler avere 'il suo colore' — in mano di lei diventava una vera 'platitude'.

> So my poor prose — faulty, tormenting and tormented as it may be, so as to have 'a colour all its own' — emerged from her hands a pure platitude.

More detailed discussion of these matters will follow later.

There seems to be some reason for accepting at least some of Cecchetti's criticisms in the case of the *Novelle Rusticane*. These stories, which Lawrence translated fairly rapidly as soon as he had finished his version of *Mastro-Don Gesualdo*, do not have the sustained interest of the earlier *Cavalleria Rusticana* collection: they are too fleeting, often mere genre pieces, with the exception of such more substantial tales as "Pane Nero" and possibly "Il Mistero"; and in Lawrence's translation this collection is surely not as satisfying as the other, which he translated later though the stories were written first. Here there *is* some evidence of haste, and a number of mistakes. But the main disappointment for a reader coming to this translation from the later one is that Lawrence, possibly still lacking confidence, has not created the richly personal idiom that characterises, for example, his *Cavalleria Rusticana*. Nevertheless, they illustrate certain oddities — and certain faults — and repay study in the context of this discussion of "fisonomia".

The points made by Cecchetti in relation to the translation of idioms, for example, may be amply illustrated here, with some examples:

"Il Reverendo"

1. Inchiodare nei suoi bilanci
   Nailing down in his account books
2. Col vento in poppa
   With the wind full-sail
3. Quelle labbra cucite
   His lips sewed together
4. Mangiare il pane a tradimento
   Eat the bread of a traitor
5. Senti montarsi la mosca al naso
   Felt the fly settle on his own nose

"Cos'è il Re"

6. Aver la tarantola
   Felt spiders

"Il Mistero"

7. Contento come una pasqua
   As happy as an Easter day

"I Galantuomini"

8. Un altro par di maniche
   Another pair of shoes

It is impossible to generalise about these examples, least of all by explaining them in terms of Lawrence's ignorance of Italian. In the first example, "inchiodare" means literally "to nail", and then by extension, and very commonly, "to fix with certainty". It does not explain the oddity of Lawrence's English to say that his dictionary did not include this metaphorical usage. Lawrence could have guessed, as well as deducing from the context, that this was no place for Verga to coin an arresting phrase. The same goes for the third of my examples, where the Italian phrase is as common as the English "with sealed lips" to which it corresponds. Is one to believe that Lawrence did not guess this? The last example is strangest: the Italian phrase means "another kettle of fish" but says literally "another pair of sleeves". This looks like a mistake: Lawrence may well have imagined that "maniche" were shoes, as he does in *Mastro-Don Gesualdo* as well. And the seventh example is a common expression for "as happy as the day is long". Anyone could guess this from the context: Lawrence is surely responding to the "fisonomia" of the Italian and using a characteristic idiom to enlarge the resources of his English. But my other examples are harder to justify or interpret. Examples 2, 4, 5 and 6 remain obscure. "Col vento in poppa" means "enjoying prosperity"; "mangiare il pane a tradimento" is " to enjoy what you have not earned"; the fifth phrase means "to fly into a rage" and the sixth "to be restless". If Lawrence is here striving after some kind of "fisonomia" the attempt is discredited by the fact that his English is imperfectly intelligible. It should be added that there are also instances where Lawrence will iron out one of Verga's metaphors; for "non ci vedeva più dagli occhi" ("Don Licciù Papa") he translates with strict accuracy but uncharacteristic literalism "had quite lost her senses".

Lawrence's unequivocal mistakes, already alluded to, are scattered here and there throughout these translations. A sentence like the following, for example, though it is by no means typical, is evidence of that careless revision which Cecchetti speaks of:

> all was plunged in that bottomless blackness so that it seemed as if you, what you saw was nothing but the noise of the torrent . . .

> . . . che pareva si vedesse soltanto il rumore del torrente.

The other striking piece of fractured English, which occurs at the end of "Pane Nero", is more interesting and problematic. I am not sure whether this represents careless revision or is another instance of "fisonomia" with the addition, perhaps, of an attempt at rendering the inarticulacy born of fear:

> Che sarà mai quella campana? O della mandra dei fichidindia, aiuto!

> Whatever bell is that? Oh, you with the cactus sheep, help!

The "translatorese" of this is perhaps unacceptable. There are some "dictionary" mistakes, that is, mistakes arising from insufficient or careless use of a dictionary, though these do not bulk as large as Cecchetti suggests. In "Cos'è il Re", for instance, "fare specie" means "surprise", not "bother"; "basto" is not "pole", a rather improbable object to use as a pillow, but "pack-saddle"; "bestia" refers to the mules, not to "cattle", which is the first meaning of the word but irrelevant here; and every story has two or three mistakes of this kind. The donkey in "Gli Orfani", for example, is supposed to die of "indigestion", a free interpretation of the "doglia" or pain it suffers from. Sometimes Lawrence's attention seems to wander. In "Di là del Mare", where he seems a little bored, he omits one phrase entirely and translates "passandosi le mani sugli occhi" as "she passed her hand over her lips". These errors are doubtless to be regretted, but there are not more of them than in many "professional" translations.

It would be possible to adduce further examples of that interlingua which is so interesting in all Lawrence's translations, that creative fusion of languages and cultures. At the beginning of "Il Reverendo", for example, Lawrence has "Well what do you want? He was never cut out for a Capucin friar", where the Italian phrase begins "Che volete" (like French "Que voulez-vous"), meaning "what do you expect" or "are you surprised?" The captain of the local militia becomes in Lawrence a "force captain", because in Italian he is a "captain d'armi", captain of the armed men. An antidote (for the cholera) is effectively called the "counter-poison", a literal rendering of the Italian "contravveleno". A phrase acquires an expressive un-English inversion, as here in "Cos'è il Re":

Allora suonarono le trombe e i tamburi

Then resounded the trumpets and drums.

Or a strange poeticism is brought into being by means of the unmediated transfer of an Italian word which has a different meaning in English, almost, but not quite, fitting the context — as in "The Saint Joseph's Ass":

quella vasta campagna bianca la quale fumava qua e la della polvere delle aie.

the vast white campagna which fumed here and there with the dust from the threshing-floors.

Here, "fumare" is literally "to smoke". Lawrence seems to associate it here and elsewhere — he uses the word in his fiction — with the painterly term "sfumato": Italy is indissolubly linked with the plastic arts.

This collection of short stories is only a qualified success. Few passages make such a striking impression unlike, for instance, those sections of *Cavalleria Rusticana* quoted earlier. By the time of his later translation he had discovered the idiom he was looking for: as if he had seen more and more clearly as he worked the profound kinship between Verga's community and the Nottinghamshire he grew up in, not perhaps in specific details of life so much as in the clash of Law and Love, and the almost ritualistic, heavy rhythm of existence punctuated by violence and conflict.[8] Verga's Sicilians, different as they are in many important respects from the miners and farmers of Lawrence's native Nottinghamshire and Derbyshire, have a comparable self-sufficient pride and feeling for the immediacy of the physical world, captured in

Lawrence's own writing. We may see this in, for example, the words of Jeli as he talks to his beloved horses:

> "It'll not be long before day comes; so we's'll get to the fair in time to take a good stand. Hi! — my little black beauty! tha sh'lt ha'e a new halter, wi' red tassels, for the fair; an' thee an' all, Starface."
>
> So he kept on speaking to the colts, to hearten them with the sound of his voice, in the dark. But it grieved him that the Black and Starface should go to the fair to be sold.

This is uncannily like Lawrence's own writing, the rhythm of the sentences beautifully in harmony with the mood, the narrator's voice never jarring with the dialect, but gently supporting it. Lawrence has, arguably, heightened the demotic: only a "che" where it should not be indicates dialect in the Italian original; but in this he has responded to the spirit and the mood of Verga's text. His Jeli is perhaps gentler than Verga's:

> Poco può passare a romper l'alba; pure alla fiera arriveremo in tempo per trovare un buon posto. Ehi! morellino bello! che ci avrei la cavezza nuova, colle nappine rosse, per la fiera! e anche tu, stellato!
>
> Così andava parlando all'uno e all'altro dei puledri perche si rinfrancassero sentendo la sua voce nel bujo. Ma gli doleva che lo stellato e il morellino andassero alla fiera per esser venduti.

Cecchetti's version is unobjectionable, but no more. It lacks the all-important "fisonomia":

> "It can't be long before daybreak, but we'll get to the fair in time to find a good place. Hey, my good Morellino! You'll have a new halter, with red tassels, for the fair! and you too, Stellato!"
>
> And he went on talking to each of the colts, so that

they would take heart hearing his voice in the dark. But he felt sad that Stellato and Morellino were going to the fair to be sold.

Lawrence has the great advantage of an idiom in which he can naturally employ the pronouns "thee" and "thou"; at this point in the story it serves to convey intimacy, and later becomes of still greater significance, where Jeli's girl-friend stops using "tu" to him as a sign of her growing estrangement, afraid, as she is, that people will talk. This matter of pronouns is important, too, at the climax of "La Lupa", where the wolf-woman tells the soldier-boy of her violent desire for him:

—Te voglio! Te che sei bello come il sole, e dolce come il miele! Voglio te!

—You! I want you! Thou'rt handsome as the day, and sweet as honey to me! I want thee, lad!

The switch from "you" to "thou" is vibrant: in Verga's text it is effected with La Lupa's first word, since she has used the "voi" form until now. Another characteristic feature of the passage from "Jeli il Pastore" in Lawrence's translation is the Englishing of the names of the horses, so that "morellino", the diminutive of "morello", "blackish" or "nearly black", becomes "my little black beauty", while "stellato" is rendered as "Starface". Lawrence also Englishes weights and measures, which are antique Sicilian in Verga, so that people are paid, for example, in guineas, like the Nottingham miners. Verga might not have approved. In a letter to Rod (December 1881) he writes:

Salma — misura antica siciliana. Questo ed altri vocaboli che non hanno il corrispondente nella lingua francese sarebbe meglio lasciarli in italiano.

Salma — old Sicilian measure. This and other terms which have no equivalent in French are best left in Italian.

But his advice was not always good. In the same letter he advises that the ever-recurring "ficodindia" should be identified by its Italian name in the French text, because it is "caratteristico": the constant concern with "fisonomia". There seems no good reason for not translating "ficodindia" as "cactus" or "prickly pear", otherwise an English reader needs a footnote, even if a French reader does not.

Phrases in Lawrence's translation of the *Cavalleria Rusticana* stories constantly delight by an inevitable rightness of idiom. In "Jeli" for instance, "cosi bella e graziosa come sei!" becomes "when you're that pretty and taking, like you are!"; while Cecchetti is content with "as beautiful as you are", the meaning of which is somewhat obscure. Again, " 'O cos'hai?' gli domandava lui" becomes " 'Why, what's a-matter wi' you?' he asked her", and in Cecchetti's version: "What's wrong? What's the matter?", which can be faulted on grounds of accuracy as well as on grounds of authenticity. Cecchetti, as I have said, censures Verga's "long and rambling" sentences, but Lawrence sticks quite close to them: and indeed they do seem to serve a purpose, that of tracing the contours of a thought or feeling, or of evoking a world of "sensations rather than thoughts". In "Rosso Malpelo" we find this:

> . . . e la vedova rimpiccoli i calzoni e la amicia, e li adatto a Malpelo, il quale cosi fu vestito quasi a nuovo per la prima volta, e le scarpe furono messe in serbo per quando ei fosse cresciuto, giacche rimpiccolirsi le scarpe non si potevano, e il fidanzato della sorella non ne aveva volute di scarpe del morto.

The sentence runs on with a kind of cruel obtuseness. There is no pity for the boy, and the final "scarpe del morto" is particularly chilling. Lawrence translates:

> . . . and the widow cut down the breeches and the shirt to fit Malpelo, who was thus for the first time dressed good as

new, and the shoes were put aside to keep until he was big enough, since you can't cut shoes down, and the sister's young man didn't want a dead man's shoes.

This has all the heartlessness of Verga's Italian, because Lawrence has followed the "logic" of the argument in Verga's own inexorable syntactic pattern. One sentence in Verga becomes three in Cecchetti, with a considerable loss of effectiveness, and some details are missed in addition:

The widow made the pants and the shirt smaller for Malpelo, who was thus dressed in almost new clothes for the first time. Only the shoes had been put aside for him until he would be big enough, since you can't make shoes smaller, and his sister's fiancé hadn't wanted the dead man's shoes.

"As good as new", "you can't cut shoes down", "the sister's young man", seem little points in Lawrence's favour; "a dead man's shoes" is, alas, not justified by the Italian.

Lawrence's rendering of idioms and proverbs is open to different interpretations, as in the case of the *Novelle Rusticane*. It is easiest simply to list some representative instances, following Verga's Italian with first Lawrence's translations and then Cecchetti's:

"Cavelleria Rusticana"

1. "Passò quel tempo che Berta filava."
   "Ah well, the time's gone by when Bertha sat a-spinning."
   "The good old days are gone."

2. "Voglio fargliela proprio sotto gli occhi a quella cagnaccia."
   "I'll show that bitch summat, afore I've done."
   "I'll get even with her right under her eyes, the dirty bitch."

"Jeli il Pastore"

3. "Dove la malaria si poteva mietere."
   "Where the malaria was so thick you could mow it."
   "Where you could mow malaria."
4. "te lo pagherebbe salato assai."
   "he'd give 'em you hotter than you fancy."
   "he'd sure pay you, but good."
5. "Se lo mangiavano cogli occhi."
   "They were wild about him."
   "They devoured him with their eyes."

"Rosso Malpelo"

6. "nondimeno era conosciuto come la bettonica."
   "at the same time he was as well known as the dandelion is."
   "nonetheless, his name was a household word."
7. "non ne avrebbe fatto osso duro."
   "would never have made old bones."
   "would never have hardened to the job."
8. "Il povero Ranocchio era più di la che di qua."
   "Poor Frog was almost gone."
   "Poor Frog already had one foot in the grave."

"Pentolaccia"

9. "Egli aveva voluto sposare la Venera per forza, sebbene non ci avesse ne re ne regno."
   "He had wanted to marry Venera at any cost, though she hadn't a thing to bless herself with."
   "He had wanted to marry Venera at any price, though she had neither king nor kingdom."

It would be hard to draw any general conclusions from these examples, least of all to the effect that Lawrence was ignorant of Italian. In the first example, he has kept a distinctive idiom, the literal meaning of which is given by Cecchetti. He has done more or less the same thing in the sixth example, where a common Italian idiom becomes something strange and powerful in English. In both cases Lawrence's version has more life than Cecchetti's, as it does in the fourth example, where Lawrence has supplied exactly the right equivalent for "salato". Examples 2 and 7 are mistakes on Lawrence's part: in the second of them he has clearly been misled by an idiom which seemed to approximate to an English idiom but in fact meant something rather different. The fifth, eighth and ninth examples show Lawrence radically altering the original: in 5, indeed, one might have supposed the first version to be Cecchetti's, the second Lawrence's. When the phrase "se lo mangiavano cogli occhi" recurs in "Rosso Malpelo" Lawrence translates it word for word, according to his established practice. In the third example he has adopted the dangerous practice of trying to clarify his author's text.

Once again the Italian language has left its mark on Lawrence's English, as is the case outside his translations as well. In "Jeli il Pastore" the phrase "scorazzava su pei greppi del monte" is rendered "went scouring away to the tops of the hills"; "Il sangue cramai e tutto una peste" is "Your blood is full of pest"; and the end of the story is very powerful in Lawrence's designedly half articulate Italianate English, a Poundian kind of intentional translatorese:

> — Come! — diceva — Non dovevo ucciderlo nemmeno? . . .
> Si mi aveva preso la Mara! . . .
> "Why!" he said. "Didn't I have to kill him? . . . If he'd taken Mara from me! . . . "

Cecchetti, who often seems to want to polish Verga's rough diamonds, makes it less forceful: " 'What!' he said. 'I shouldn't even have killed him? . . . But he'd taken Mara! . . . ' "

There can be no doubt that Lawrence has made some mistakes: in "Jeli" the horse stands "colle froge al vento", "his nostrils in the wind", and Lawrence substitutes "chin" for "nostrils"; in "The How, When, and Wherefore", where Lawrence's attention wanders, for identifiable reasons, there are dozens of small errors of this kind. But as I have already noted, some of the "mistakes" Cecchetti notes are surely nothing of the kind. He calls attention, for example, to the following passage:

> The sun touched the high rocks of the Hill of the Cross, the grey puffs of the olive-trees fumed upon the twilight . . .

> Il sole toccava le roccie alte del Pioggio alla Croce, le chiome grigie degli ulivi sfumavano nel crepuscolo . . .

and objects to the Lawrentian "fumed", already referred to, as if it were a gratuitous poeticism. But in his own version he translates "chiome" as "foliage", where in fact it is a more literary word, "tresses" or "plumes".

"The How, When, and Wherefore" is the least well translated of the whole collection; it is in Verga's "Frenchy" manner, Maupassant with a dying fall, and Lawrence does not bring the same imaginative sympathy to it as to the other tales. He responds best to the intermittent ironic humour, but elsewhere grows impatient, excising phrases or ignoring them, as one might expect from his brusque dismissal of this aspect of Verga's work in his introduction to his *Cavalleria Rusticana* collection, and his scornful remark about the "sophistications of the city life of elegant little ladies". This is all in keeping with the Verga "myth" (to which Verga himself did not necessarily subscribe) of the fusion of the modern and Homeric, so important to Lawrence. The highly sophisticated, rather world-weary man of letters emerges in this story, as he does in "Fantasticheria", and in the introduction to "Gramigna's Lover", where the Sicilian world is distanced in a fashion unacceptable to Lawrence. *The How, When, and Wherefore* becomes for Lawrence just another instance of what he classifies disparagingly, via Maeterlinck, as "the treasure of the humble", false and sentimental populism rather than homage to the Law. Verga certainly makes an emphatic bid for sympathy here:

> The tenacious attachment of those poor people to the rock on which fortune has left them, while sowing princes here

and duchesses there, this courageous resignation to a life of hardship, this religion of the family, which reflects on to the occupation followed, on to the house, and on to the stones which surround it, seem to me — perhaps for a quarter of an hour — most serious and worthy of respect.

Lawrence doubtless has a point when he claims that Verga is not writing at his best when he is writing in this "compassionate" vein, and he does not do so in *Rosso Malpelo* or *Jeli il Pastore* for example. But Verga is not so unequivocally committed to his myth as Lawrence is, and does not try to convince himself that his modern sensibility can shed its contradictions in the "primitive" world he has evoked.

NOTES

1. J. H. Whitfield, *A Short History of Italian Literature* (London: Penguin, 1961).
2. Introduction to *Cavalleria Rusticana* (*Phoenix One*, 1936).
3. Giovanni Cecchetti, 'Verga and D. H. Lawrence's Translations', *Comparative Literature*.
4. There are some useful observations on dialect in literary texts in Norman Page, *Speech in the English Novel* (London: Longman, 1973).
5. Victor Shklovsky, 'Art as Device', in *Russian Formalist Criticism: Four Essays*, ed. L. T. Lemon and M. J. Reis (University of Nebraska, 1972).
6. Giovanni Verga, *Lettre al Suo Traduttore* (Florence: 1954).
7. Cf. J. N. R. Saunders, *D. H. Lawrence and Italy*, unpublished B. Phil. thesis, especially Chapter 3.
8. Cf. Lawrence's *Study of Thomas Hardy*, (*Phoenix One*, 1936).

3 Lawrence and Verga: *Mastro-Don Gesualdo* (with a note on Grazzini's *Dr Manente*)

The journey from Sicily to Ceylon that Lawrence and Frieda undertook in February and March 1922 was a kind of holiday for them. Lawrence describes the RMS *Osterley* in terms that might have been borrowed from the satirical idiom of Bunin's *Gentleman from San Francisco*:

> At 8 o'clock the breakfast gong rings and such a menu — cooked pears, porridge, fish, bacon, eggs, fried sausages, beefsteak, kidneys, marmalade, all there. Then afterwards one sits about, flirts or plays croquet. Eleven o'clock comes the steward with a cup of Bovril. One o'clock lunch — soup, fish, chicken or turkey, meat, entrees, always much too much. Four o'clock tea. 7 o'clock dinner. Ah no, one eats all the time.

But Lawrence still found time to work on the translation of Verga's novel *Mastro-Don Gesualdo*, his first translation from the Italian. By March the novel was finished, truly, as Cecchetti says, incredible speed for a work so strange and challenging in idiom, which Verga himself described as representing "una difficoltà enorme" for the translator. It is unfortunate that this should have been Lawrence's first encounter, as a translator, with Verga, since he was clearly working in conditions unconducive to work and with very little in the way of reference books to hand. It is probably his least satisfactory translation, with numerous awkwardnesses and obscurities, some glaring errors, and (more seriously) no sign of that overall control which the best of the short story translations have. Moreover, Lawrence does not seem to have the confidence to carry off the interlingual effects of the *Cavalleria Rusticana* stories: so that where the Italian shows through, the effect is often merely clumsy:

> La casa della baronessa era vastissima, messa insieme a pezzi e bocconi, a misura che i genitori di lei andavano stanando ad uno ad uno i diversi proprietari, sino a cacciarsi poi colla figliuola nel palazzetto dei Rubiera e porre ogni cosa in commune: tetti alti e bassi; finestre d'ogni grandezza, qua e la, come capitava; il portone signorile incastrato in mezzo a facciate da catapecchie. Il fabbricato occupava quasi tutta la lunghezza del vicoletto.

> The house of the Baroness was vast, added together by bits and pieces, according as her parents had ousted one by one the various proprietors, until they had installed themselves at last with their daughter in the mansion of the Rubiera's, and joined in everything common: roofs high and low; windows of every size, here and there, as it happened; the great door of the nobles set in the middle of a lot of hovel-fronts. The building occupied almost the whole length of the street.

Even if "joined in everything common" is merely a printing error, this writing is surely cramped, not liberated, by the matrix of the original. Awkwardness of this kind is often accompanied by obscurity or inaccuracy, as here, for example:

> "Poi," aggiunse il marchese, "questi sono militari per modo di dire; come io ho fatto il voto di castità perche sono cavaliere di Malta."

> "But then," added the Marchese, "these fellows are just so-

to-speak soldiers, like me who have taken the vow of chastity by way of being a Knight of Malta."

The punctuation, but not the other oddities, may be explained in terms of printing errors. There are also some instances of obscurities arising from Lawrence transferring images which he has probably not understood:

Non vorrei che giuocassimo a scarica barile fra di noi.

I don't want us to play at empty-the-barrel between ourselves.

Don Diego is described at one point as having a "cardboard face", for "faccia di cartapesta", a papier-mâché face like that of a puppet: in Chapter 7 Lawrence translates this correctly, where two personages are "like papier-mâché figures", but he did not go back to correct his earlier mistake, which betokens haste. Neri's reproach to Bianca, whom he has seduced and dishonoured — "Credi che non ti voglia piu bene?" — is weakened by being inaccurately translated as "Do you think I'm not fond of you?" instead of "Do you imagine that I don't love you any more?" Lawrence is not above misreading a tense, as where "si sciugava il sudore col fazzoletto" becomes "one can wipe one's sweat on one's handkerchief", or letting his attention wander: so "Io ne parlo per sentita dire" becomes "I ask because I want to know" instead of "I can only talk about it from hearsay." Again, " 'Un momento!' esclamò il canonico balzando in piedi" becomes " 'One moment!' exclaimed the cannon-priest, dancing to his feet." Here, apart from the curious "cannon-priest", Lawrence has misread "balzare", "to jump", as "ballare", "to dance". He reads "cosa" for "cosi", and translates "lutto" by "quarrel", as though it were the French "lutte", when in fact it means "mourning". He embraces *faux amis* in other contexts, too: for "Era uno squallore pel paese" he writes "All the village was in squalor", not knowing that "squallore" is "gloom";

"strologare , which in context means "to study", becomes "to astrologise": though this practice can lead, as in the short stories, to interlingual felicities, as when "inviperito" is translated as "viperish" when it is not much more than "enraged", or "mingherlino", meaning "frail" — L'amoroso, un mingherlino che lei si sarebbe messo in tasca — is rendered as "mingy".

If Lawrence's knowledge of Italian is not quite up to the task, his ear for idiomatic speech often stands him in good stead in this early translation as in his later ones. In Chapter 1 there is a striking little instance of this when the house catches fire and the old, sick Don Ferdinand shouts in panic, "come un'anitra", "like a duck", "Di qua! di qua!", and Lawrence keeps the duck-noise by translating it as "Quick! up here! Quick! up here!" although there is no word for "quick" in Verga's text. He had done something similar again at the end of Chapter 3, where the sentence "le scarpaccie di Alessi e di Rosario che accorevano a rotta di collo" is translated: "the clattering shoes of Alessi and Rosaria who came running to break their necks"; there is no word in the original for "clattering" but the sound of the Italian words may be held to justify the addition. And at moments Lawrence breaks into Nottingham dialect, where his finely attuned ear has caught the hint of dialect in Verga's text, as, for example, in the moving conversation between Gesualdo and Diodata. Diodata, who to Gesualdo is merely the woman about the house, even though she has borne his children, feels deep love for him; but in the course of his tragic progression from "mastro" to "don" he disposes of her along with the other trappings of his peasant past. Gesualdo's awkward attempt at tenderness and sincerity as he blunders on, telling her that it is time for him to marry, and at the same time asking her uncomprehendingly, or not quite honestly, why she is so sad, is beautifully rendered in the dialect that Lawrence often uses in his own novels (especially *Lady Chatterley's Lover*) as a magic language of intimacy: though here there is an ironic contrast between the special sanction peculiar to the idiom, and the facts of the relationship:

> "Thou'rt a good lass! — good and true! and careful with
> thy master's things thou'st always been . . . I'm only talking
> now for the sake of talking — because thou'rt fond of me.
> I'm not thinking of it yet awhile. But one day or the other
> I shall have to give in, I suppose — Who have I worked and
> starved for, then? — I've got no children — "
>   Then he saw her face, bent down to earth, very white
> and wet with tears.
>   "What art crying for, silly?"
>   "Nothing, your honour! — So! — Don't take any notice."
>   "What had ta got in they head, tell me."
>   "Nothing, nothing, Don Gesualdo."

Gesualdo's betrayal is made that much crueller by being expressed through a language which is, on the surface at least,
more delicate than Verga's Italian:

> "Perchè piangi, bestia?"
> "Niente, vossignoria! . . . Cosi! . . . Non ci badate . . . "
> "Cosa t'eri messa in capo, di'?"
> "Niente, niente, don Gesualdo . . . "

As far as the translation of idioms is concerned, it is once
again difficult to generalise about the principles governing
Lawrence's practice. Sometimes he opts for the closest English
equivalent:

> "Ho troppa carne al fuoco"

> "I've got too many irons in the fire"

and sometimes he translates word for word and obscures the
meaning:

> "in punta di forchetta"
> "on the end of his fork"

— the idiom means "affectedly", which perhaps Lawrence knew, since five pages later he translates the same phrase as "in such a mincing fashion": another sign of haste, perhaps. Sometimes when he is trying to carry over an idiom for the sake of "fisonomia" his ignorance lets him down:

"e senza cercare il pelo nell'uovo" ("Without splitting hairs")

"And without looking for the skin in the egg"

where Lawrence has obviously misread "pelle", skin, for "pelo", hair. Even weirder things happen. The idiom "Non ho peli sullo stomaco!" is translated as "I've not got the feelings of a horse!", although the idiom actually means "I'm not unscrupulous". At one point Lawrence even coins an earthy Sicilianism; for "spendere l'osso del collo" he writes "spend the very blood out of his veins" (in the place of, as the original has it, "spend the bone from one's neck"). Lawrence is writing English in a Sicilian spirit (cf. the Italianate dialogue of *The Lost Girl*). "Spent the eyes out of his head" is another that Lawrence renders word-for-word, to the annoyance of Cecchetti, who insists that it is as common in Italian as "spend every last penny" is in English. But such an objection refuses to take cognisance of the problem of "fisonomia", which cannot be resolved (any more than any other problem of style) by an appeal to "standard" usage.

It may be said that Lawrence secularises Verga's text to a certain extent. The trappings of Catholicism are perhaps unfamiliar, or even uncongenial; certainly the language of religion which remains vestigially in Verga's style is a very different matter from the Nonconformist language of self-scrutiny that marks Lawrence's. It is hard to say how much force remains in Verga's religious idioms, which certainly appear inevitable, almost reflex forms of address and reference. The noun "un christiano" means little more than "a human being"; Lawrence pays no special attention to it, or to the oft-repeated "grazia di Dio", as in

"un bel pezzo di grazia di Dio anch'essa"

"[she was] also a fine piece of goods"

"si inghiottava in pace un po' di grazia di Dio"

"they could at least swallow in peace a bit of nourishment"

"Pensi solo a mangiare! . . . Ci vuol la grazia di Dio!"

"You think of nothing but eating! . . . It takes some providing!"

"Che non ne mangiate grazia di Dio?"

"Don't you eat good food, don't you?"

All these instances of the expression seem to retain at least some overtone of "God's bounty" in the Italian which has been consciously removed in translation (at any rate, near the end of the book, when the priest in his anger is described as being "fuori della grazia di Dio", one assumes that the phrase has not become altogether automatised). This is the kind of problem that Verga foresaw when writing to Rod; he gave his French translator virtually *carte blanche*, even allowing him to make whatever cuts he considers necessary: "So I don't have to tell you that I approve and endorse everything you have to do to make the text intelligible to French readers, in those passages which are characterised by *couleur locale*, too. Let me know, moreover, what cuts you consider necessary . . . " So sure was he of being hardly translatable that he was even prepared to sacrifice his ironic title, and make the book just *Don Gesualdo*. Lawrence resolved that particular problem in his introductory explanation.

II

THE STORY OF DR MANENTE

Lawrence concludes his Preface to *The Story of Dr Manente*
with a characteristically elliptical note on the author:

> "Lasca" means "roach", or some such little fish like that.
> It was the nick-name of Anton Francesco Grazzini, who
> was born in Florence in March 1504, just twelve years
> after the death of Lorenzo the Magnificent, which took
> place in 1492. Lasca arranged his stories, after the manner
> of Boccaccio, in three Suppers, and *The Story of Dr
> Manente* is the only one we have complete of the third and
> last Supper. The stories of the Second Supper and those of
> the First Supper will occupy two volumes following on
> this one, and in the final volume will be included a study
> of Lasca, his life and his work.

This was Lawrence's last published translation from the
Italian, brought out by the Florentine publisher Orioli, who
also printed *Lady Chatterley's Lover*. Warren Roberts records
that in the autumn of 1928 Lawrence had suggested to Orioli
a series of Italian Renaissance novelists in translation; shortly
afterwards he wrote to the OUP with a similar proposal. The
series as such came to nothing, although Orioli followed up
Manente with other books by Lawrence, including *Apoca-
lypse* and *Last Poems*. Lawrence's translation was probably
finished in the summer of 1928, and Orioli published it in
March 1929. As I have said, the volume attracted little attention.

In his preface to *Mastro-Don Gesualdo* Lawrence had written that "subjectivity is largely a question of the thickness of
your overcoat". Introspection, he claimed, was a northern
phenomenon, and the colder the climate, the more intense
the self-preoccupation (the Russians and the Swedes were
held to demonstrate the truth of this curiously positivistic

theory). Thus the distinctively "democratic" vision of late nineteenth-century literature was also a northern phenomenon; with the "hero" discredited, writers made every man his own hero, with the "heroism" turned inwards on the "coruscations" of the "soul". The Italians, a race without overcoats (so the argument runs), had swallowed an alien vision by adopting the styles and subject-matter of democratic realism with which they had no vital connection:

> The main motive, the gross vision of all the nineteenth century literature, is what we may call the emotional-democratic vision or motive. It seems to me that since 1860, or even 1830, the Italians have always borrowed their ideals of democracy from the northern nations, and poured great emotion into them, without ever being really grafted by them. Some of the most wonderful martyrs for democracy have been Neapolitan men of birth and breeding. But none the less, it seems a mistake: an attempt to live by somebody else's lights.

It goes without saying that one should not visit Turin or Milan in winter without a fairly thick overcoat; but these arguments, however specious in themselves, are a part of Lawrence's Italian myth. In the early essay, *David*, he uses similar antitheses to characterise the impact of the Renaissance in Italy, the moment at which he locates, in his Hardy . study, the displacement of Law by Love:

> Adam, David, Venus on her shell, the Madonna of the Rocks; they listen all of them. What do they hear? Perpetual sound of waters. The level sweep of waters, waters overwhelming. Morality, chastity — another world drowned: equality, democracy, the masses, like drops of water in one sea, overwhelming all outstanding loveliness of the individual soul. Quenching of all flame in the great watery passivity which bears down at last so ponderous . . . Yet no final surrender. David, with his knitted brow and full limbs,

is unvanquished. Livid, maybe, corpse-coloured, quenched with innumerable rains of morality and democracy. Yet deep fountains of fire lurk within him. Must do. Witness the Florentines gathered at New Year's night to watch that fiery fruitless orgasm. They laugh, but it is Leonardo's laugh. The fire is not ridiculous. It surges recurrent. Never to be quenched. Stubborn. The Florentine.

This is where Grazzini fits into Lawrence's vision of the Italian Renaissance, and it explains why Lawrence should have found him so attractive. For tradition has it that Michelangelo's statue has an orgasm every New Year, and the Florentines turn out to watch the spectacle, to jeer and admire. The joke is like a "beffa" played on the self-consciously beautiful David by the admiring and cynical townsfolk. Thus the ideal is brought down to earth, the pure embodiment of Spirit reduced to a basic law of Flesh. Lorenzo the Magnificent (it is not irrelevant that Lawrence was familiarly known as, and even signed himself, Lorenzo) played a "beffa" on Dr Manente, who had become too self-important, by spiriting him away and giving out that he had died of plague, so that when after many tribulations he made his way back to Florence, the townsfolk thought he must be a ghost — even his wife, who was pregnant by another man. The ordeal brings out the best in him: he does not whine but displays what Lawrence (who identifies with both Manente and Lorenzo) calls "courage and force of life", and the attitude to the "beffa" of those involved is "tough without being hard-boiled". In this way the carnivalesque episode recounted by Grazzini is enlisted to support Lawrence's opposition to the subjective individualism of modern culture. We need Manente's courage, says Lawrence, in this age of self-pity when "we are so sorry for ourselves that we have to be soothed by art as by candy. Renaissance art has some of its roots in the cruel "beffa" . . . Michelangelo stuck his languishing Adam high on the Sistine ceiling for safety, for in Florence they'd have played a rare "beffa" . . . "

Lawrence's characterisation of Grazzini as "of the day and

of the city . . a local and temporal writer" is supported by this story. It is fairly unsubtle, sometimes racy, but also with dull and styleless patches. Lawrence translates with few mistakes, and seems quite committed to his task, after a rather graceless beginning. He is sometimes made unhappy by the formal deliberateness of the Italian, and tries to loosen its syntax, with somewhat awkward results:

> It is a joke played by the Old Lorenzo de' Medici on a doctor, one of the most brazen men in the world, as you will soon see; and such novel things happened, and such complications ensued, such strange events took place in the course of this jest, that if ever you were staggered and amused, this time you're going to be.

> Una beffa fatta dal Magnifico Lorenzo vecchio de' Medici ad un medico de' piu prosontuosi del mondo, come tosto intenderete. Nella quale tanti nuovi accidenti intervennero, tanti vari cosi naquero, tanti strani avvenimenti occorsero, che, se mai vi maravigliaste e rideste, questa volta vi maraviglierete e riderete.

The role of master of ceremonies does not come easily to Lawrence, and he evidently dislikes the flamboyant showmanship of this passage. Thus he prunes syntactically and provides the incongruous and awkward "this time you're going to be" to supply a needed kind of "raciness". This is consistent with Lawrence's underemphasis of the stylish arrogance of Lorenzo: thus the old monk who impersonates Manente, for example, who is "allegrissimo di far la voglia del Magnifico", is described as "chuckling in his obedience to the orders of the Magnifico", which makes him more amiable than he really is: likewise the grotesque exaggerations in physical details (for example, the description of the monk's gown, "quella zimarracia", and his hat, "quel cappelone", are rendered just quaint in Lawrence's "with that old gown hugged round him, and that old hat". Lawrence partly conceals the fact that Grazzini's jest is somewhat too deliberate by means of an emphasis on local colour and the syntactical simplifications already mentioned. These may be observed in a more extended passage which reveals Lawrence's characteristic emphasis on action and the concrete:

> . . . e ravviluppatogli il capo, quasi di peso lo condussero in quel salotto; e postolo sopra il letto a sedere, non gli avendo ancor cavato le manette, lo lasciarono stare; e usciti di quindi, se n'andarono in camera del Guardiano, dove per suo comandamento vennero subito due conversi, accioche, veggendo, imparar potessero quel tanto che egli avessero a fare nel governare e dar mangiare a maestro Manente, non ostante che dal Magnifico ne avessero avuto particolarmente avviso.

> Having muffled up his head again, they half carried him to that sitting-room, and having put him on the bed, they left him with the handcuffs still on, and went to the Father Superior's room. There, two lay brothers were at once brought so that they might see and learn what they had to do about minding and feeding Doctor Manente, although they had received strict orders from the Magnificent.

The two languages undeniably operate within different syntactic patterns, but even allowing for this it is clear that Lawrence has revised Grazzini. Sometimes he makes open, apparently rather impatient, cuts:

> . . . della qual cosa tutti coloro che udiendo, insieme col Magnifico, avevano fatto le maggior maraviglie e le maggiori risi del mondo; ne per lo molto meravigliarsi e ridere che avessero fatto: non si potevano contenere di non si meravigliare e di non ridere.

> When those present with the Magnificent had marvelled and laughed, and marvelled and laughed consumedly, and still could not stop marvelling and exploding with laughter, Lorenzo . . .

and Lawrence launches into a condensed version of the next sentence. Lawrence is notably uncritical of his great Renaissance namesake in his *Movements in European History*, and his sympathy for him has something in common with that rather unpleasant approval of the flogging in the essay on *Two Years before the Mast* in *Studies in Classic American Literature*. Yet here, as a translator, Lawrence manifests a certain impatience with the world of the "beffa" and its deliberate cruelty, even while praising it.

4 Koteliansky and Bunin's Gentleman

On 16 June 1921 Lawrence writes to Koteliansky:

> My dear Kot: Yesterday *The Gent. from San Francisco*
> and the pen: very many thanks. Have read *The Gent.* —
> and in spite of its lugubriousness grin with joy. Was Bunin
> one of the Gorki-Capri crowd? — or only a visitor? But it is
> screamingly good of Naples and Capri: so comically like
> the reality: only just a trifle too earnest about it. I will
> soon get it written over: don't think your text needs much
> altering. I love a "little carved peeled-off dog" — it is too
> good to alter.

As we have seen, Lawrence had already worked with Koteliansky, on the Shestov version, and perhaps on other texts.[1]
Koteliansky, for his part, had helped Lawrence in various
ways, particularly by getting manuscripts typed. Koteliansky's
English, it is clear, was not altogether fluent or idiomatic, and
he understandably did not feel equal to seeing through his
translations of Bunin without some assistance. As he was
aware of Lawrence's unwillingness at this time to become
known as a translator he may have been reluctant to approach
him, and must already have made overtures to Leonard Woolf,
who was in the end responsible for the other three stories in
the collection; but this one took Lawrence's fancy, for reasons
which I shall examine, and he was doubtless glad to help out
a man whom he respected and for whom he felt a lasting
friendship. The Koteliansky manuscript of the first version of
the translation seems not to be available: so one can only

guess at the extent of Lawrence's involvement in the final version; but it must surely have been considerable. Leonard Woolf's comment in a letter of 13 September 1967 bears this out.[2] "A little carved peeled-off dog", for example, is undeniably a colourful rendering of "krokhotnuyu, gnutuyu, oblezluyu sobachku", but no one would claim that it was accurate, and it was finally *not* found "too good to alter": the *Dial* text prints "a tiny, cringing, peeled-off little dog", and the Hogarth text "a tiny, cringing, hairless little dog", which is very much closer to what Bunin wrote. One can only speculate about the frequency of occurrence of such passages which "did not need much altering". The extent of them may, however, be guessed at by the fact that Lawrence took half the profits, albeit under protest, when *The Dial* published the story, as a letter of 24 December 1921 records: "I got the cheque for £12 – odd. I *wish* you would let it be ¼ for me – I am not justified in taking half – the *Dial* should have paid you *more*, also."

Another two letters in which Lawrence refers to *The Gentleman from San Francisco* and his part in the translation are worth citing. The first (14 January 1922) records Lawrence's displeasure at *The Dial's* naming him as co-translator, as well as his satisfaction with the story as it was printed (in the first edition of the book of Bunin stories, Lawrence was *not* named, though his name was added on an erratum slip). The other letter, of 9 July 1922, mentions this volume: "My dear Kot: I had your letter, and the Bunin book next day . . . What a pretty cover Bunin has! But the tales are not very good: *Gentleman* is much the best. Some of Woolf's sentences take a bit of reading. Look at the last sentence on p. 71."[3] Possibly this smacks of self-praise, yet I think that Lawrence is right to call attention to the fact that Woolf has not reworked Koteliansky's version in sufficient detail or with sufficient boldness. The sentence which Lawrence is alluding to, cited here, is not untypical:

Perhaps, too, there was in her soul a drop of purely feminine pleasure that here was a man to whom she could give her small commands, with whom she could talk, half seriously and half jokingly as a mentor, with that freedom which their difference in age so naturally allowed — a man who was so devoted to her whole household, in which, however, the first person — this, of course, very soon became clear — was for him, nevertheless, she herself.

The intention is doubtless Jamesian, but the execution falls far short of the model.

It would be hard to demonstrate any temperamental affinity between Lawrence and Bunin, despite some superficial points of similarity: indeed, in many respects the Russian author represented values to which Lawrence was opposed. An émigré, who left the Soviet Union in 1921 and lived abroad, largely in Paris, until his death in 1953, Bunin may be called the last representative of the Chekhovian short story tradition, and as such was taken up by representatives of the Bloomsbury intelligentsia with whom Lawrence had serious intellectual differences. He employs a complex ironic narrative method, like Chekhov, but with more of a self-indulgent morbid pessimism than is generally to be found in Chekhov's work. He is at his most characteristic in stories of thwarted and frustrated love, where his writing is marked by a kind of lurid suffocating eroticism, especially prevalent in his later collections. Lawrence hit on a slightly uncharacteristic tale, in that the wit is keener and the human concern more central than in much of his writing. The other three stories proposed for translation by Koteliansky did not, as he said, give him much pleasure. But if *The Gentleman from San Francisco* is not altogether typical Bunin, it shows a remarkable grasp of the potentialities of Russian prose. In its descriptive writing it exploits the capacity of the Russian language for building up huge, static, verbless syntactic units, where the only dynamic principle is the tension generated between the strings of inflected nouns and their accompanying adjectives. Of course Lawrence could not have known this at first hand, since his knowledge of Russian probably never reached even a minimal passive level; but it is reasonable to suppose that he could sense it in Koteliansky's evidently very Russianate English, and in the stories translated by Leonard Woolf it remains very clearly. As in the *Manente* translation, though for different reasons and thus with different results, Lawrence has evidently become impatient with the clogged texture of Bunin's writing, so opposite in method and manner to the improvisatory parataxis characteristic of Lawrence's own work in this period; this is particularly clear in the last, somewhat overwritten, satanical-mystical section.

Yet one should remember that *The Gentleman from San Francisco* made Lawrence "grin with joy"' There is no doubt that he felt committed to this translation, and was not simply obliging a good friend when he undertook it. The letter of 16 June already provides some clue as to why this should be so: "Was Bunin one of the Gorki-Capri crowd? — or only a visitor? But it is screamingly good of Naples and Capri." The short-lived Gorky cult was at its height in radical intellectual circles: Lawrence was thus out of sympathy with Gorky. Still less did he like the fashionable cultural refuge of Capri, which he had visited only eighteen months before. A letter from Capri, dated 5 February 1920, runs as follows:

> I am very sick of Capri: it is a stewpot of semi-literary cats — I like Compton Mackenzie as a man — but not as an influence. I can't stand his island. I shall have to risk expense and everything, and clear out: to Sicily, I think. One gets to Palermo in twelve hours by steamer from Naples. So I think we shall go. My luggage hasn't come yet — I heard of it from Turin. But come what may, I must clear out of this Cat-Cranford of Capri: too much for my nerves. No, I don't want to do a satire. It all just dries up one's bowels — and that I don't like — I shall go and find a place in Sicily.

Mordant satirist as he was on occasion, satire was not a mode that came naturally to Lawrence, and he seems to have wel-

comed Bunin's story as the kind of critique of Capri he might
have wished to produce himself: he could thus express his
feelings vicariously. The focal point of Bunin's tale is not
where Lawrence himself might have placed it: the only "semi-
literary cats" in Bunin's story are the Russian émigrés, self-
mockingly presented: "There were other arrivals too, but
none worthy of notice: a few Russians who had settled in
Capri, untidy and absent-minded owing to their bookish
thoughts, spectacled, bearded, half-buried in the upturned
collars of their thick woollen overcoats." But it is not the
Capri writers that Bunin is concerned with. In his somewhat
overemphatic and (as Lawrence says) earnest way he is tackling
in a small compass the very large theme, also dear to Lawrence,
of the stranglehold of the machine on modern life and modern
consciousness. A paragraph from (for example) Lawrence's
essay *Climbing down Pisgah* might serve as a gloss on the
moral scheme and ideological import of Bunin's story:

> Let us scramble out of this ash-hole at the foot of Pisgah.
> The universe isn't a machine after all. It's alive and kicking.
> And in spite of the fact that man with his cleverness has
> discovered some of the habits of our old earth, and so lured
> him into a trap; in spite of the fact that man has trapped
> the great forces, and they go round and round at his bidding
> like a donkey in a gin, the old demon isn't quite nabbed.
> We didn't catch him napping. He'll turn round on us with
> bare fangs, before long. He'll turn into a python, coiling,
> coiling till we're nicely mashed. Then he'll bolt us.

Bunin's gentleman, at the start of the story, is taking two
years' holiday from his particular ash-hole:

> He was fully convinced of his right to rest, to enjoy long
> and comfortable travels, and so forth. Because, in the first
> place he was rich, and in the second place, notwithstanding
> his fifty-eight years, he was just starting to live. Up to the
> present he had not lived, but only existed; quite well, it is

true, yet with all his hopes on the future. He had worked
incessantly — and the Chinamen whom he employed by
the thousand in his factories knew what that meant.

The Gentleman has put off living for too long — he no longer
knows how to. He sees nothing of the beauty of southern
Italy and Capri, which Bunin evokes by juxtaposing it with
the shabby-elegant hotels of the milieu in which the Gentleman belongs. When at last he dies of a heart attack, his body
is carried off in the steamer, the powerfully evoked creature
of the machine, menaced by a vengeful demon:

> Through the snow the numerous fiery eyes of the ship
> were hardly visible to the Devil who watched from the
> rocks of Gibralter, from the stony gateway of two worlds,
> peering after the vessel as she disappeared into the night
> and storm. The Devil was huge as a cliff. But huger still
> was the liner, many storeyed, many funnelled, created by
> the presumption of the New Man with the old heart.

The somewhat ornamental diablerie is more reminiscent of
Forster than akin to Lawrence, and this is one of a number of
points at which the ultra-sophisticated Bunin makes his points
with a certain heavy-handedness. The passages in which he
attempts to invoke the natural simplicity of the Italian
peasants likewise fall short of the intended effect of spontaneity and contrast unfavourably with Lawrence's own Italian
travelogues, though he has been scrupulously faithful to Bunin:

> The pipers bared their heads, put their pipes to their lips:
> and there streamed forth naive and meekly joyous praises to
> the sun, to the morning, to Her, Immaculate, who would
> intercede for all who suffer in this malicious and lovely
> world, and to Him, born of Her womb among the caves of
> Bethlehem, in a lowly shepherd's hut, in the far Judean
> land . . .

— such writing smacks of a quite un-Lawrentian fancifulness.

But there are other elements which are curiously "Lawrentian" in the common associations of the term. The mysterious figure of the Asiatic Prince, the necessary counterweight to the mechanical Gentleman, is an element of the Lawrentian kind, even if his attraction to the daughter of the Gentleman is more conventional than such relationships tend to be in Lawrence's own work:

A new passenger appeared on board, arousing general interest. He was a hereditary prince of a certain Asiatic state, travelling incognito: a small man, as if all made of wood, though his movements were alert; broad-faced, in gold-rimmed glasses, a little unpleasant because of his large black moustache which was sparse and transparent like that of a corpse; but on the whole inoffensive, simple, modest. The daughter of the Gentleman from San Francisco stood side by side with the Prince, who, by a happy circumstance, had been introduced to her the previous evening. She had the air of one looking fixedly into the distance towards something which he was pointing out to her, and which he was explaining hurriedly, in a low voice. Owing to his size, he looked amongst the rest like a boy. Altogether he was not handsome, rather queer, with his spectacles, bowler hat, and English coat, and then the hair of his sparse moustache just like horse-hair, and the swarthy, thin skin of his face seeming stretched over his features and slightly varnished. But the girl listened to him, and was so excited that she did not know what he was saying. Her heart beat with incomprehensible rapture because of him, because he was standing next to her and talking to her, to her alone. Everything, everything about him was so unusual — his dry hands, his clean skin under which flowed ancient, royal blood, even his plain, but somehow particularly tidy European dress; everything was invested with an indefinable glamour, with all that was calculated to enthral a young woman.

The word "glamour" is invested with more than its common-place significance in relation to the charisma of the Prince as perceived by the girl: there is a transcendence of novelette conventions strikingly reminiscent of some of Lawrence's own work, especially, as it happens, in this period and the Mexican years. Curiously, the Soviet edition of Bunin, which is on the whole close to the first edition, omits the Russian phrases which catch this charismatic quality most vividly: "though his movements were alert", and "to her, to her alone". The only difference between the Hogarth text and the *Dial* text in this passage is the substitution of "low voice" for "reduced voice" in the later printing, which rather suggests that Lawrence was still concerned about the naturalness of his version, so close as it originally was to the Russianism of Koteliansky's English.

There was, then, a personal drive behind Lawrence's translation of Bunin, as was the case with all his other translations, and once again a detailed comparison of Lawrence's version with the original throws an interesting light on both, since the translation constitutes a kind of critique. Regrettably, there is no way of knowing, as with the Shestov translation, exactly what Koteliansky's version looked like. Given the fact that this is once again a translation at two removes, how-ever, it is remarkably faithful at the verbal level and remark-able free from mistakes. The *Dial* text and the Hogarth text may be equated for all practical purposes, though it is interesting to note that in the later text the punctuation is considerably heavier, breaking up the long sentences; an important half-sentence has disappeared, too, though this is doubtless an oversight: Tiberius lost his head not just, as the Hogarth text has it, "from the absurdity of such power" but also "out of fear lest death should stab him from behind". But as far as sheer mistakes are concerned, I have located only three. Lawrence translates "gogotali" as "giggled", in the sentence "where gigantic furnaces roared and dully giggled", though this is probably a misreading of a manuscript at some stage (the Russian word is really "roared" as with laughter, though the translation "gurgled" may have been misread). A little later, Lawrence writes of Chinese boys with "girlish thick eyebrows", where the Russian word (resnitsy) means "eyelashes". The Russian phrase "podbezhal k samoy dveri", "ran right up to the door", is rendered "went to the very door", doubtless a slip of Koteliansky's. But it is clear enought that these small errors are of no great importance: much more noteworthy is the high degree of accuracy possible even when, as here, a translation is undertaken by two writers in collaboration, one of whom does not know the language: a common enough practice nowadays, and one which has often produced very impressive results.

There are much more interesting points of divergence unconnected with accuracy as such. Radical differences between Bunin's text and Lawrence's result from intrinsic dissimilarities between the structures of English and Russian. Bunin exploits the massiveness of Russian inflexions, with his strings of adjectives in oblique cases piling up, perhaps with participles and adverbs, resolving on to a noun only at the end of a huge period. This is a stylistic device which, while proper to Russian, does not transfer happily into English, as the Koteliansky/Woolf texts show. Lawrence's prose is, by a conscious choice of the translator, airier and more rapid. In part, as I have said, he simply punctuates more frequently, making half a dozen sentences out of one. But there are other far-reaching changes which it is instructive to consider in detail. On page 6 of the Hogarth text, for example, there is a description of the steamer in the storm:

> The steamer trembled in every fibre as she surmounted these watery hills and struggled with the storm, ploughing through the moving masses which every now and then reared in front of her, foam-crested.

The writing is energetic by virtue of the fact that it throws an emphasis upon the verbs: trembled, surmounted, struggled, reared. This ship has a very good chance of survival. But the effect of Bunin's Russian is quite different:

Параход весь дрохал, одолевая и её, и эти горы, точно плугом разваливая на стороны их зыбкие, то и дело вскипавшие и высоко взвивавшиеся пенистыми хвостами громады.

Following the syntactic pattern exactly, the Russian, put into pidgin English, would run somewhat as follows:

> The steamer all trembled, overcoming both it, and these hills, as if with a plough churning to the sides their rolling, now and then boiling and high-lifting-themselves in foamy tails masses.

Here the emphasis falls not on the purposeful activity of the ship in fighting a way through the heavy seas, but on the mass of the participles that threaten to swamp it: and the passage has a massive sonority, in addition. This is not an isolated instance of Lawrence radically reforming his original: a similar process may be observed on page 18 of the Hogarth text in a passage describing the progress of the Gentleman and his family up the Capri hillside from the landing-stage to the hotel:

> past the stakes of the vineyards and wet, sturdy orange-trees, here and there protected by straw screens, past the thick glossy foliage of the brilliancy of orange fruits.

That odd nominalisation ("brilliancy") betrays the influence of the Russian syntax. The Russian is as follows:

среди кольев на виноградниках, полуразвалившихся каменных оград и мокрых, корявых, прикрытых кое-где соломенными навесами апельсиновых деревьев, с блеском оранжевых плодов и толстой глянцевитой листвы.

or, in pidgin English:

> Among the stakes in the vineyards, half-ruined stone

walls and damp, rough, covered here and there with straw
screens orange trees, with the sheen of orange fruit and
thick glossy foliage.

Here the difference in pace between the English and the
Russian is even more striking. Bunin's travellers are held back
and make slower progress, encumbered as they are and hin-
dered by the dense old plantations, the natural prodigality of
which impedes their dash for the familiar comfort of the hotel.
In Lawrence's translation the journey is too swift, too easily
accomplished. The ease is apparent from the initial slight misreading of Russian "sredi", literally "among", as "past", and
the effect is reinforced when Lawrence chooses to repeat the
word. The crumbling stone walls, an additional obstacle as
well as a reminder of Nature's power to assert herself precisely
where man has staked his claim, have vanished from Lawrence's
landscape (a rare instance of oversight, which may, of course,
have been Koteliansky's: they are absent from the *Dial* text
too). The sensation of greater rapidity and more purposive
movement is reinforced by the fundamentally different
word-order of the English. As the adjectival phrase piles up
in the Russian, it seems actively to obscure the orange trees,
which we come to only after an effort. In Lawrence's version
the fruit shine out nakedly, defying the thick foliage; in Bunin's
original they remain obscurely swathed. Something essential to
Bunin's effect has been lost; and however impressive Lawrence's
prose may be in its own terms, an essential level of irony — that
fatalistic Romantic irony that runs through Bunin's work —
has been much reduced. Two more examples may serve to
reinforce my point. One is from page 32, describing the dawn
on the day when the Gentleman's body leaves Capri:

. . . as the blue sky of morning lifted and unfolded over
Capri, and Monte Solaro, pure and distinct, grew golden,
catching the sun which was rising beyond the far-off blue
mountains of Italy . . . "

The Russian is:

> когда поднялось и раскинулось над островом Капри голубое
> утренее небо и озлотилась против солнца, восходящего за
> далёкими синими горми Италии, чистая и чёткая вершина
> Моите-Соляро.

Again Lawrence's syntax is clearer and simpler. In Russian, however, the mountain makes a more portentous and dramatic appearance:

> when rose up and spread itself above the island Capri the
> blue morning sky and turned gold against the sun, rising
> beyond the distant blue hills of Italy, the clear and sharply-
> outlined peak of Monte-Solaro . . .

Bunin's elaborate stylistic contrivance has been expunged. Evidently, in its own terms, Lawrence's description has merit — "Monte Solaro, pure and distinct, grew golden" — but the dramatic irony inherent in Bunin's syntax has been lost.

As a final example I would cite page 32, where the author describes the driver of a cart who

> . . . kept flogging his wiry small horse that was decorated
> in Sicilian fashion, its harness tinkling with busy little bells
> and fringed with fringes of scarlet wool, the high saddle-
> peak gleaming with copper and tufted with colour.

In Russian this is:

> . . . хлестал свою крепкую лошадку, по-сицилиански
> разряхенную, спешно громыхаюшую всяческими
> бубенчиками на уздечке в цветных шерстяных помпонах
> и на остриях высокой медной сёделки

or, word by word:

> he whipped his strong little horse, in the Sicilian way
> adorned, hurriedly rumbling [the term is often applied to

heavy vehicles] with all kinds of little bells on the bridle in coloured wool pompons and on the edges of the high bronze harness-pad.

The relation between bells, pompons, bridle, and saddle is exact in the Russian, but Lawrence splashes colour indiscriminately; the elaborate possibilities in Russian inflexions for describing the relationship between objects has been sacrificed to the analytic practicality of English.

In this passage, we may notice the somewhat un-English "wiry small horse": the explanation for it is doubtless to be found in the Russian diminutive "loshadka", a "small horse" in one word; Russian, like Italian, is rich in expression diminutives. As with the translations from Italian, but less frequently, a non-English locution or word-order has had a significant role in Lawrence's style. On page 2, for instance, we find:

Carnival he thought of spending in Nice, in Monte Carlo, where at that season gathers the most select society . . .

for the Russian

Karnival on dumal provesti v Nitse, v Monte-Karlo, kuda v etu poru stekaetsa samoye otbornoye obshestvo . . .

Sometimes the habit of inverting subject and predicate emerges as poeticism, probably unwitting: "pechal'ny byli evo ogni" is "sad seemed the lights"; "sladko pakhnet v Italii zemlya posle dozhdya" is "sweetly smells the earth in Italy after rain"; sometimes the effect is grotesque, as when "vysokuyu, udivitel'novo slozheniya blondinku" becomes "a tall, wonderful figure, blonde", though this is doubtless a vestige of Koteliansky. More interesting is the passage on page 25 where the Gentleman is pleasurably anticipating Carmella's forthcoming dance:

The Gentleman from San Francisco got up hastily, pulled

his shirt-collar still tighter with his tie, and his abdomen tighter with his open waistcoat, settled his cuffs, and again examined himself in the mirror . . . "That Carmella, swarthy, with her enticing eyes, looking like a mulatto in her dazzling-coloured dress, chiefly orange, she must be an extraordinary dancer," he was thinking.

The Russian, at the point of the Gentleman's reflections, runs as follows:

. . . эта Кармелла, смуглая, с наигранными глазами, похохая на мулатку, в цветистом наряде, где преобладает оранжевый цвет, пляшет, долхно быть, необыкновенно.

or in a pidgin transcription:

That Carmella, swarthy, with her enticing eyes, like a mulatto, in a bright outfit, where an orange colour predominates, dances, surely, remarkably.

In fact Lawrence's version of these disorganised thoughts is more pidgin than my pidgin-literal version, and much odder than the Russian, since in the original there is an effect of cohesion given by the grammar which works against the incoherence of the Gentleman's thoughts. There is no equivalent of "in her dazzling-coloured dress, chiefly orange", and the verb for "to dance" relates back without strain to Carmella. Lawrence's version is, however, undeniably successful. Another point at which Lawrence's English has an effectively foreign ring is on page 15: "A heavy fog hid Vesuvius to the base, and came greying low over the leaden heave of the sea, whose waters were concealed from the eye at a distance of half a mile." The "foreign" element lies in the expression "came greying"; the Russian reads "nizko serel nad svintsovoi zybyu morya", using a very characteristic Russian colour verb (in Russian grass can "green").

In smaller details, too, Lawrence's translation rejects complete literalness, though it creates particular effects by means of a kind of creative mimicry. Whatever may be lost by the greater raciness and rapidity, there is throughout Lawrence's translation a sense of the creative energy of a writer warming to his task. This is the kind of creativity that can translate such a phrase as Bunin's crucial "Shli oni — i tselaya strana, radostnaya, prekrasnaya, solnechnaya, prostiralas' pod nimi" as "they descended, and the whole land, joyous, was sunny beneath them" — not an exact equivalent, but exactly right in its quasi-Biblical resonance of joy ("was sunny"). As in the case of Lawrence's translations from Italian, his creative insight into his original would be hard to rival. It is a matter for regret that Lawrence did not collaborate further with Koteliansky: George Zytaruk has described Koteliansky's work as a translator, and it is an impressive achievement, but there is a strong case for claiming that a creative writer is best translated by another creative writer.

NOTES

1. Cf. George J. Zytaruk, *The Quest for Ranamin*.
2. "Koteliansky's English was remarkable and had to be considerably revised. When we translated with him, he wrote out his translation first in double spacing and we then translated it into English. I am sure Lawrence must have done something of the kind." Letter from Leonard Woolf to the present author, 13 September 1967.
3. See Zytaruk, op. cit.

Lawrence and Bunin: An Appendix

In 1921, when Lawrence was working on his translation of *The Gentleman from San Francisco*, he was also engaged in revising an early short story called "The Thimble" (published in the American magazine *Seven Arts* for March 1917). This somewhat gauche tale deals with a theme that was to preoccupy Lawrence greatly in his major fiction, the theme of the irreparable damage sustained by the English psyche and English civilisation in the First World War. In this story, as in other works by Lawrence, the old world is shown to have (in Lawrentian terms) come to the verge: but the symbolic resonances of this large theme are more than the fable will bear. The principle character is Hepburn, who comes home from the war to his very English wife, terribly disfigured as a consequence of an accident: "it seems that it was a shell fired by one of our own fellows, and it hit me because it was faultily made." The accident underlines the theme of the hollowness of the ideals for which men fought, so that the collapse of a civilisation, produced by the war, is understood in terms of a failure within it. Hepburn's injury is paralleled by the neurasthenic exhaustion of his wife, who has had pneumonia, and is equally a victim of the war. In her long wait for Hepburn's return, she has discovered a thimble under the cushions of her sofa: she cannot remember seeing it before, but Lawrence uses it to stand for a continuity with an older and more secure mode of domestic life, which is also, he suggests, felt now to be an onerous anachronism: "It was large, too, big enough for her. It must have been some woman's embroidery thimble, some bygone woman's, perhaps some Lady Amber-syth's. At any rate, it belonged to the days when women did stitching as a usual thing. But it was heavy, it would make one's hand ache.''

This theme is developed when Hepburn appears and the couple try to maintain a pretence of normality. The impossibility of doing so is emphasised in the most tangible fashion by the fact of Hepburn's disfigurement:

"What are you doing? What have you got?" asked the mumbling, muffled voice. A pang went through her. She looked up at the mouth that produced the sound. It was broken in, the bottom teeth all gone, the side of the chin battered small, whilst a deep seam, a deep, horrible groove ran right into the middle of the cheek. But the mouth was the worst, sunk in at the bottom, with half the lip cut away.

The continuity symbolised by the thimble is seen as an intolerable pressure from the past on a radically changed present: as Hepburn asks her about it, a "film of separateness" comes over her. When Hepburn acknowledges his wound, and the irrevocable change that it symbolises, there is some hope of a new start:

"And do you think we've got the power to come to life again, now we're dead?" she asked.
"I think we have," he said.
There was a long pause.
"Resurrection?" she said, almost as if mocking. They looked slowly and darkly into each other's eyes. He rose unthinkingly, went over and touched her hand.

Hepburn throws the thimble out of the window, and a whole way of life goes with it. The ending is hopeful: too hopeful, indeed, and schematic. Lawrence seems to have recognised that the story is sentimental and seriously flawed, but he returned to it and used it as the basis of a masterly tale, "The Ladybird". By the time he came to write this later story, he had decided that the Hepburns were beyond salvation, or at any rate could not resolve the contradictions of their civilisation so easily. The "man who died" and came to life again would be drawn from the margins of society. In some of Lawrence's later fiction he is an outcast; here he is Count Dionys, the Bohemian aristocrat who owes more than a little to Bunin's Asiatic Prince. This sketchy but significant character in Bunin's tale is described at length:

> He was a hereditary prince of a certain Asiatic state . . . a small man, as if all made of wood, though his movements were alert . . . a little unpleasant because of his large black moustache which was sparse and transparent like that of a corpse . . . Owing to his size, he looked amongst the rest like a boy . . . Altogether he was not handsome, rather queer . . . and then the hair of his sparse moustache just like horse-hair, and the swarthy, thin skin of his face seeming stretched over his features and slightly varnished . . . Everything about him was so unusual — his dry hands, his clean skin under which flowed ancient, royal blood, even his plain, but somehow particularly tidy European dress.

Something of the same life-in-death quality emerges in Lawrence's description of Johann Dionys Psanek, the "aboriginal", "fire-worshipping" aristocrat from the East (Lawrence has used for his name the Czech word "psanec", an outlaw, which he transcribes wrongly). Psanek lies close to death as a prisoner-of-war in an English hospital:

> It was Count Johann Dionys Psanek, a Bohemian . . . He was a small man, small as a boy, and his face too was rather small. But all the lines were fine, as if they had been fired with a keen male energy. Now the yellowish swarthy paste of his flesh seemed dead, and the fine black brows

seemed drawn on the face of one dead . . . The black hairs
came out of his skin thin and fine, not very close together.
A queer, dark aboriginal little face he had, with a fine little
nose: not an Aryan, surely . . . His face seemed to Daphne
curiously hidden beneath the black beard, which nevertheless was thin, each hair coming thin and fine, singly, from
the sallow, slightly translucent skin . . . his moustache
made a thin black line round his mouth . . . He was still
carefully dressed in the dark blue uniform, whose shabbi-
ness could not hinder the dark flame of life which seemed
to glow through the cloth from his body.

The Asiatic Prince's brief power over the (very) European
daughter of the Gentleman, in Bunin's story, is taken up, in
"The Ladybird", in the relationship of Psanek and Daphne
(who is Hepburn's wife from 'The Thimble" with an admix-
ture of the daughter from the Bunin tale — "she was so purely
an English blonde, an Aphrodite of the foam" . . . "sorrow,
pain, thwarted passion had done her great damage"). This
new Dionysus from the East, a member of those "curious
little aboriginal races of Central Europe", carries a spirit of
outlawry into the ruined world of English domesticity:
" 'Psanek means an outlaw; did you know? . . . I will not be
Johann Dionys any more. I will be Psanek. The law has shot
me through.' " And he rises from his death-bed to accomplish
the resurrection of which Hepburn was incapable. The thimble,
in this version, is his, and Daphne will use it to sew fine silk
shirts for him. Basil, the Hepburn figure with a touch of
Middleton Murry, advocates a more spiritual kind of "resurrection through love": having "been through the ordeal, you
arrive at a higher state of consciousness, and therefore of life.
And so, of course, at a higher plane of love . . . The war has
opened another circle of life to us — a wider ring." Daphne
chooses Psanek's way, the way of the "dark gods" (significantly, until she meets him, the only man she felt drawn to
was a gamekeeper: thus the story is linked to *Lady Chatterley's Lover*).

There is then a slight but unmistakable influence of Bunin on Lawrence: or rather a motif in the Russian writer served to catalyse elements already active in Lawrence's imagination. This translation, like the translations of Shestov, Verga, and Grazzini, took its place in the constant process of writing and rewriting by which Lawrence's work was linked to his life and his changing sympathies and antipathies.

Conclusion

I began by defining my topic as a study of a minor part of a major *oeuvre*, and I would like to end by underlining this. In the last analysis, Bunin and Lawrence have little in common. And although there is a more interesting kind of kinship between Lawrence and Verga, it is nevertheless clear that Verga's stories had little influence on Lawrence's work. We know that Lawrence had reservations about Verga's methods:

> *Cavalleria Rusticana* and *La Lupa* have always been hailed as masterpieces of brevity and gems of literary form. Masterpieces they are, but one is now a little sceptical of their form. After the enormous diffuseness of Victor Hugo, it was perhaps necessary to make the artist more self-critical and self-effacing . . . Maupassant's self-effacement becomes more blatant than Hugo's self-effusion. As for the perfection of form achieved — Mérimée achieved the highest, in his dull stories like *Mateo Falcone* and *L'Enlèvement de la Redoute.* But they are hopelessly literary, fabricated. . . . [Verga] has clipped too much away. The transitions are too abrupt . . . We need more looseness. We need an apparent formlessness, definite form is too mechanical. We need more easy transitions from mood to mood and from deed to deed. A great deal of the meaning of life and art lies in the apparently dull spaces, the pauses, the unimportant passages. They are truly passages, the places of passing over.

These "places of passing over" (the phrase has characteristic religious vibrations) are essential to Lawrence's shorter fiction, as to his longer, and they do indeed have little place in Verga's. In "The Prussian Officer", for example, a story in which there is an emotional clash between two men even harsher than in "Cavalleria Rusticana", their relationship is explored in the course of a long route-march by means of flash-back and by the use of the scorched countryside as a correlative. The transition from the first manifestations of the officer's sadism to the killing, in the course of eighteen pages, is accomplished by means of a constant interaction between objective description and psychological analysis so that changes in consciousness themselves become events, as they seldom do in Verga's tales. It is the same process of shifting point of view between internal and external planes that makes the violent conclusion of *The Fox* plausible within such a short compass.

But if one cannot demonstrate any very substantial gain, for Lawrence's work, by virtue of his activity as a translator, what I have said already may suggest that as texts in their own right Lawrence's translations are creative work of a high order. Dryden, one of the earliest and still one of the most stimulating theorists of translation, stressed the obligations of the translator as regards what he called the "maintaining the character of an author, which distinguishes him from all others, and makes him appear that individual poet whom you would interpret". The "character" resides not only in the content but in the form of a writer: indeed, there is no reason to suppose that "content" and "form" are any easier to separate in the case of translation than they are in any other area of literary study. Matthew Arnold remarked, in his long essay *On Translating Homer*, that: "To suppose that it is fidelity to an original to give its matter, unless you at the same time give its manner; or rather to suppose that you can give its matter at all, unless you can give its manner, is the mistake of our pre-Raphaelite school of painters." In Lawrence's translations matter and manner are fused by virtue of the fact that he recognises an obligation to the creative individuality of the *language* of his source text. Pasternak, himself a fine translator, commented that the greatest joy of a work of art was its unrepeatability: how, then, he asked, can a translation repeat it? The "fisonomia" on which Verga insists is precisely that creative distinctiveness which Lawrence's versions, by the means analysed, achieve. By stretching the resources of English Lawrence accomplishes more than Verga had hoped for, when he wrote to Rod, advancing what were surely counsels of despair:

> Farete bene a sopprimere o a sostituire quei proverbi che sono intraducibili in francese, e quegli incidenti legati dal "che", caratteristici in siciliano, ma che anche nell' italiano formarono la mia disperazione quando intrapresi questo tentativo arrischiato di lasciare piu che potevo l'impronta del colore locale anche allo stile del mio libro.

You would do well to suppress or find substitutes for those proverbs which can't be translated into French, and for those strings of events introduced by "che", a typical feature of Sicilian, but which even in Italian drove me to distraction when I made this foolhardy attempt, which was beyond my powers, to leave an imprint of local colour on the very *style* of my book.

It was this challenge which Lawrence rose to so impressively.

Select Bibliography

PRIMARY SOURCES

Original Texts

Bunin, Ivan, *Gospodin iz San-Frantsisko* (Paris: Imprimerie Union, 1920).

Grazzini, Francesco, *Le Cene di Anton Francesco Grazzini detto Il Lasca* (Florence: G. C. Sansoni, 1890).

Shestov, Lev, *Apofeoz Bezpochvennosti* (St Petersburg: 1905).

Shestov, Lev, *Sur les confins de la vie* (*L'Apothéose du Depaysement*), (Paris, 1927).

Verga, Giovanni, *Mastro-Don Gesualdo* (Mondadori: Milan, 1940).

Verga, Giovanni, *Novelle Rusticane* (Turin: F. Casanova, 1883).

Verga, Giovanni, (Vita dei Campi) *Cavalleria Rusticana ed altre novelle* (Milan: Mondadori, 1892).

Lawrence's translations

Bunin, Ivan, tr. S. S. Koteliansky and D. H. Lawrence, *The Gentleman from San Francisco. The Dial* (January 1922); and in *The Gentleman from San Francisco and other stories* (London: Hogarth Press, 1922).

Grazzini, A. F., tr. D. H. Lawrence: *The Story of Dr Manente, being the tenth and last story from the suppers of A. F. Grazzini called Il Lasca* (G. Orioli, Bookseller, at 6, Lungarno Corsini, Florence, 1929).

Verga, Giovanni, *Mastro-Don Gesualdo*, tr. D. H. Lawrence (New York: 1955) (reprinted from the plates of the first edition published by Seltzer).

Verga, Giovanni, *Little Novels of Sicily*, tr. D. H. Lawrence (London: Blackwell, 1929).

Verga, Giovanni, *Cavalleria Rusticana*, tr. D. H. Lawrence (London: Cape, 1928).

Shestov, Leo, *All Things are Possible*. Authorised translation by S. S. Koteliansky with a foreword by D. H. Lawrence (London: Secker, 1920).

SECONDARY SOURCES

Chambers, Jessie, *Lawrence, D. H., A Personal Record* (London: Cape, 1935).

Gordon, D. J., *D. H. Lawrence as a Literary Critic* (New Haven and London: Yale UP, 1966).

Lawrence, D. H., *The Tales of D. H. Lawrence* (London: Heinemann, 1934).

Lawrence, D. H., Studies in Classic American Literature (New York: Doubleday, 1955).

McDonald, Edward D. (ed.), *Phoenix: The Posthumous Papers of D. H. Lawrence* (London: Heinemann, 1936).

Roberts, Warren and Moore, Harry T, (eds.), *Phoenix Two* (London: Heinemann, 1968).

Moore, Harry T. (ed.), *The Collected Letters of D. H. Lawrence* (London: Heinemann, 1962).

Saunders, J. N. R., "D. H. Lawrence and Italy", unpublished B. Phil. thesis (Oxford: CUP, 1967).

Steiner, George, *After Babel* (London: Queens UP, 1975).

Zytaruk, George J., *The Quest for Rananim* (Montreal/London: McGill, 1970).

Zytaruk, George J., *D. H. Lawrence's Response to Russian Literature* (The Hague: Mouton, 1971).

In addition, I have made substantial use of Giovanni Cecchetti's work on Verga and Lawrence:

Cecchetti, Giovanni, "Verga and D. H. Lawrence's Translations", *Comparative Literature*, Vol. IX, No. 4 (Fall, 1957).

Verga, Giovanni tr. Cecchetti *The She-Wolf and Other Stories* (Berkeley and Los Angeles: Univ. of California, 1962).

Other articles consulted include:

Arnold, Armin, "D. H. Lawrence, the Russians, and Giovanni Verga", *CLS*, Vol. 2, No. 3 (1965).

Wasiolek, Edward, "A classic maimed: *The Gentleman from San Francisco* examined", *College English*, Vol. XX (1958).

Index